What is happening to religion in Australia?

With church attendance in Australia at an all-time low, the Christian churches have lost their influence in secular Australia. The shocking revelations of child sexual abuse in Christian institutions are only part of the reason for this paradigm change. Philip Hughes' deep dive into wide-ranging research shows how changes in society itself have impacted the churches, and offers some suggestions as to how the churches might re-connect with the Australian community. This is an indispensable book for all Church leaders.

Dr Muriel Porter OAM
Melbourne writer, historian and lay Anglican

Philip Hughes is one of Australia's foremost scholars of religious change. In his new book, *What is happening to religion in Australia?*, he draws on his extensive research experience, peerless expertise with survey and census data, deep reading and perceptive personal insights to deliver a compelling and highly readable account of Christianity's changing fortunes. Accessible and engaging, this is the best book of its kind I have read on Australian religion. I highly recommend it to anyone interested in how faith is shaped by society and culture.

Professor Andrew Singleton
Professor of Sociology and Social Research
Deakin University, Geelong

Philip Hughes has an uncomfortable habit of reminding Australia's churches that the number of people who identify as Christians has been declining for a longer period than we may care to admit.
What is happening to religion in Australia? might be uncomfortable reading, but it deserves careful reading by Christian leaders trying to wrestle with the decline of Christianity in Australia. Hughes' reputation as a religious demographer underscores the urgency of the statistical analysis offered here.
Not every answer offered by *What is happening to religion in Australia?* to the 'Why? How? What next?' questions will be equally convincing to every reader. However, be that as it may, the questions posed here are unlikely to disappear any time soon.

Rev. Associate Professor Darrell Jackson
Principal, Whitley College, University of Divinity

Understanding
the trends

What is happening to religion in Australia?

Philip Hughes

Published in Australia by
Coventry Press
33 Scoresby Road
Bayswater VIC 3153

ISBN 9780648982272

Copyright © Philip Hughes 2025

All rights reserved. Other than for the purposes and subject to the conditions prescribed under the *Copyright Act*, no part of this publication may be reproduced, stored in a retrieval system, or transmitted in any form or by any means, electronic, mechanical, photocopying, recording or otherwise, without the prior permission of the publisher.

Catalogue-in-Publication entry is available from the National Library of Australia
http://catalogue.nla.gov.au

Cover design by Ian James – www.jgd.com.au
Text design by Coventry Press
Set in EB Garamond

Printed in Australia

Contents

Acknowledgments xi
Introduction xiv
Chapter 1: The Trends: What is Happening 1
    Experience 2
    The 2021 Census 6
    Information from surveys 10
    Other religions 14
    International trends 17
    In summary 20
Chapter 2: Understanding the Trends 21
    Secularisation 21
    Differentiation 22
    Identity 29
    Denominational identity 33
    In summary 35
Chapter 3: The Change in Personal Values 38
    From duty to family life to personal fulfilment 38
    Values in production and people 46
    Duty and personal fulfilment 49
    Spirituality 52
    Has the decline in church involvement produced a moral vacuum? 53
    In summary 56
Chapter 4: Changes in Society's Values 58
    Social values and social cohesion 58
    Tolerance of diversity 60

Constraints to avoid harming others	61
Equality of opportunity	62
Homophobia	63
What does this have to do with secularisation?	64
The environment	70
Serving the community	71
In summary	73
Chapter 5: Immigration and Secularisation	**75**
The roles of religion in the immigration process	75
The impact of immigration on the religious profile	77
Second generation immigrants	82
The pro-family values of immigrants	83
In summary	85
Chapter 6: Why Some Denominations are declining Faster than Others	**86**
Why are the most tolerant churches declining most rapidly?	86
Distinctness from society	89
The charismatic revival	94
The decline of the progressive churches	98
In summary	102
Chapter 7: How People Find Meaning Today	**104**
Beyond religion	104
Spiritual but not religious	106
Civic religion	114
The sources of meaning	117
In summary	121
Chapter 8: How Should Churches Respond?	**123**
A new Axial Age?	123
How churches should and should not respond	128
The importance of children and youth	134
Characteristics of being church	137

Resources for nurturing the spirit and creating
    community 141
References 147
Data used and referred to in this book 153
Additional reading 154

Acknowledgments

This book came about because of a comment following a presentation. Dr Muriel Porter was in the audience and suggested that my presentation be made into an 'easy-to-read' book. She suggested that the material would help church leaders and others interested in the Christian faith to understand what is happening and to respond more effectively. She offered to help me with a book. Her encouragement, her assistance in the planning of the book and in reviewing my manuscript are deeply appreciated.

Another friend has offered extensive comment. Prof. Robert Cramb has been a close friend for more than 50 years. We were both involved in the Christian Union at Melbourne University in the early 1970s, and then in involvement in the first church of which I was appointed a minister. As I have valued our sharing of ideas over many years, I have valued his critique and input into this book.

Another friend, Dr Bob Dixon, has also provided critical comments and corrections to the book. Bob Dixon was the founder and long-time director of what is now called the National Centre for Pastoral Research, a research body responsible to the Catholic Church in Australia. He worked closely with me through his role on the board of the Christian Research Association.

In many ways, this book arises from a great variety of experience as both a minister in three churches and a member of others, and as a researcher who has worked across churches of all denominations and with people of other faiths. Many people have contributed to these experiences. I pay particular tribute to those people with whom I have worked in research: to other staff and board members in the Christian Research Association. For 11 years, I worked with a joint NCLS and Edith Cowan University research team and am particularly grateful to Dr Peter Kaldor and Prof Alan Black for working with them on issues of church decline, spirituality and community.

Some of the material that has made its way into this book has been in previous books, chapters and articles. In particular, the census data used in this book was previously published by the Christian Research Association in my book *Australian Religious and Non-Religious Profiles: Analysis of the 2021 Census*. Other ideas have appointed in articles in *Pointers*, the quarterly bulletin of the Christian Research Association. I continue to appreciate the opportunity the Christian Research Association has given me to explore these themes and analyse the relevant data over 40 years.

Over the past eight years, I have been supervising nine doctoral students, first through Harvest Bible College, and then through Alphacrucis University College. I have also had one doctoral student at the University of Divinity. All the doctoral studies were in the area of religion and society. The process of supervision has assisted me to think through the themes that are presented in this book and I am grateful for what I have learnt from my students and through their own studies. Some of their work is explicitly quoted or mentioned in this book. Other work that is not explicitly mentioned has also contributed to my thinking.

At an international level, I have been grateful for the opportunity to attend many conferences of the International Society for the Sociology of Religion. Conversations with Prof. David Voas and with Prof. Ryan Cragun in the 2022 conference in Taiwan, as well as reading their books and articles, have contributed to my understanding of the international context. I have also appreciated Dr Peter Brierley and the Lausanne International Researchers Network which he formed and supported for many years. He continues to feed us all with valuable research.

Over my 50 years of post-graduate studies and ministry, my wife, Hazel, has been my closest companion. Apart from reading my numerous books and articles and correcting my many typographical, spelling and grammatical errors, she has shared and supported the personal side of the story represented in this book. For that support, I am most grateful.

While many have contributed to my thinking, this book is the result of my own thinking and does not represent the views of any of the individuals or organisations mentioned above. We live in complex changing times and, in the light of our experiences and our analysis of the situation, people may well come to different conclusions about the nature of the changes, what has caused them and how to respond to them. Over the years, I have certainly changed in my own thinking. I encourage readers to examine the material I present here carefully and critically. As we honestly share our understanding, so we are best placed to make this world a better place.

Philip Hughes

Introduction

The rapidly changing fortunes of the Christian churches in Australia – now only about 10 per cent of people attend Christian worship with any degree of regularity – can be attributed to a range of factors. In this book, I attempt to identify and explain those factors, seeking to understand what has happened, what is happening now and how individuals and churches might respond. In particular, I analyse data from the last Australian census in 2021 and other surveys to provide as accurate a picture as possible of the situation now facing Australian Christian churches.

While secularisation has a long history rooted in the Enlightenment, the recent declines in religious attendance can be traced back to the early years of the twentieth century and particularly to the years following the Second World War, as medical and technological advances, together with the growth of welfare systems, radically changed Western societies. These developments resulted in huge changes to societal values, particularly related to female fertility.

Prior to the 20th century, Western societies depended on women bearing large families to provide a sufficient workforce, compensate for high childhood mortality rates, and provide care for the elderly. But technological advances over the last 200 years have increasingly meant fewer people are needed to produce food and manage the community. Clean water supplies and effective sewerage systems, coupled with the control of common childhood diseases through vaccinations and the introduction of antibiotics and improved medical care, meant child mortality rates improved dramatically. Add the introduction of the contraceptive pill in

1961 – the first safe, effective form of contraception that women could control, and women were no longer hostage to their fertility. Sexual relationships became primarily for pleasure rather than reproduction.

With women now free to work outside the home and enter public life in significant numbers, the centuries-old structure of the family changed dramatically. The introduction of no-fault divorce in Australia in 1975 meant that people were no longer forced to remain in unhappy marriages. This, together with increasingly widespread acceptance of homosexual relationships, meant that the Christian churches' traditional teachings and rules concerning the family, women and sex were challenged or considered irrelevant. Australian adults now order their lives around their desire for personal fulfilment and happiness rather than dutiful conformity to institutions and religious codes. As people seek that personal fulfilment in diverse ways, so new values of inclusion, tolerance and consent have come to the fore as the bases for contemporary society.

These changes have massively undercut the basis of much of the churches' influence, structured for centuries around upholding the older patterns of human relationships with the expectations of conformity and obedience to authorities. The appalling evidence of child sexual abuse within churches and church organisations, so publicly revealed to wider society over the past twenty years, and universally decried, has robbed the Christian churches of the moral force they once exerted.

I will explore these issues through the following chapters. In Chapter One, the trends in religion will be outlined. In Chapter Two, I will examine the social forces which have driven these trends. Chapter Three will focus on the changes in personal values and goals which have evolved in this new more individualistic age, while Chapter Four will explore the social values which enable society to cohere in the midst of this individual approach to life. In Chapter

Five, I will explain the impact of immigration on the trends that have been identified in earlier chapters. I also note the changing patterns which are occurring in the process of immigration itself.

While the overall scene is one of declining church attendance, in some denominations, numbers are being maintained. Indeed, while some denominations have seen falling numbers since the 1970s, the Pentecostal churches have grown remarkably. These differences will be explored and explained in Chapter Six.

In Chapter Seven, I explore how individuals are responding to the changes around them and what forms the search for meaning now takes. Building on many years of research in church life, Chapter Eight explores the ways in which churches can slow the rate of decline and respond positively to this challenging environment.

The book ends with some responses to the secularised context. It suggests that this context offers new ways in which communities and individuals may find meaning in life, values to live for, and opportunities to make the world a better place.

Chapter 1

The Trends: What is Happening

The past 30 years have seen a dramatic decline in the religious beliefs and practices of Australians. A 2018 social attitudes survey – which I will explain in detail below – revealed a little more than 10 per cent of Australian adults attended Christian church services monthly or more often. This was a significant drop from 1993, when a quarter of Australians attended church. Australia is not unique. This pattern of decline has long been visible in northern Europe, but is now being identified around the world.

Between 1993 and 2018, the proportion of the population who prayed weekly or more often, halved from 38 per cent to 19 per cent. Only one quarter of Australian adults said they believed in God in the same 2018 study, with nearly half the population saying they used to believe in God but now no longer did so.

As we consider these figures, we need to note that few Australians have gone to church frequently. Since the early 19th century, only about a quarter of the population went to church with any degree of regularity. Nevertheless, whether they went to church or not, almost the whole population regarded themselves as Christian. The Censuses recorded more than 85 per cent of the population as Christian through to the 1970s.

While the changes began in the 1970s, the rate of change began to accelerate with the new millennium. The proportion of the population identifying as Christian fell to just 44 per cent in 2021, with the vast majority of those leaving the Christian faith now saying they had no religion. During the same period, attendance at Christian worship plummeted.

Experience

My experience as a Christian minister since the 1970s illustrates the changing Australian pattern. I have served as a minister of religion in three churches. Two of these churches are no longer in existence. One of those was in the inner city. I served there in the 1970s when there was a committed group of about 30 people who attended every week. Most of those people were much older than me, but we did have a group of people recently out of university who were of my own age group.

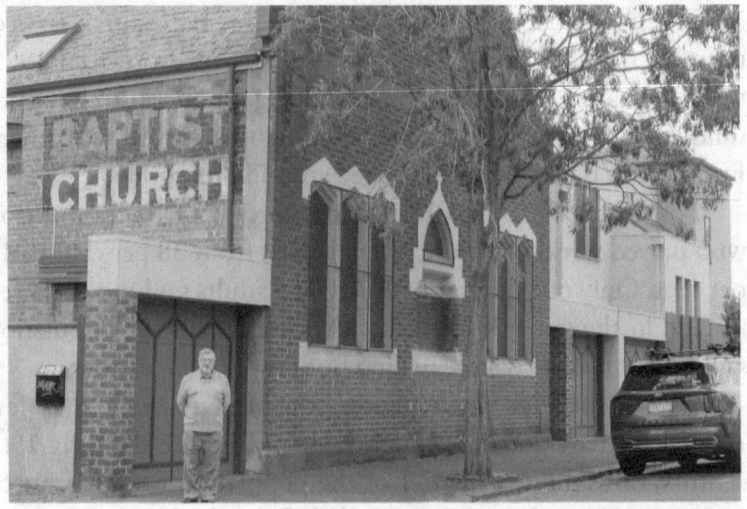

The author outside Baptist Church in inner city Melbourne now converted into housing.

I was conscious then that there were many people moving into this inner city suburb, but I did not find ways of connecting with them. They put up high walls at the entrances to their homes both metaphorically and materially. I had a strong sense that the church had to change if it were to engage these people. Somehow, the culture of the church did not connect with their culture. It was this experience which led me to the substance of my doctoral studies: how did churches relate to their cultures and to what extent was it important to reflect their cultural contexts? And to this theme, I am now returning.

In the decade after my ministry there, the church met in a café. The original church building was turned into a block of housing units. Later, the church itself closed.

My second period of church ministry was in the 1980s, after I had completed my doctorate. This was a larger church and I worked in a team with a fellow minister. We served two congregations. One was a small group of former Presbyterians who had not moved into the Uniting Church when it had been formed. I was a Baptist, but we used the old Presbyterian church and they preferred to worship with us in their old church than with the Uniting Church which was now located in the former Methodist Church. After I left, the congregation became a Presbyterian church again, but has since closed.

Baptist Church in a regional town which is now a social service centre.

The other congregation which I served at this time was in a moderately sized regional town. More than one hundred people were involved in the church, including many young families, and hence children and youth. A couple of families with no previous connection with a church joined while I was there. They were mostly people who had had significant challenges in life and for whom the church offered the possibility of a new start. However, after my time at the church, the congregation split, with members moving to churches of different denominations in the town. The church building became used as social service centre. A remnant congregation continued in a new church building on the edge of town.

My third period of ministry was with a Uniting Church in suburban Melbourne. It met in a grand building which could seat 200 people. For some of the events around the celebration of the church's centenary and on special occasions when we welcomed students from a nearby school, we filled the church. On average, we had a congregation of about 50 people. I was employed half-time, with the other half of my time being used in research. The church had assets in the form of a large hall and several houses which it had used to care for elderly women. When I went there, it was suggested by senior people in the denomination that my role might be to close the church.

While I was serving that church, I developed a scheme for providing a Christian community for young people coming from rural areas to study in the city. The students lived in church-owned houses. My one requirement of them was that we meet once a month to reflect on and re-affirm those values which made us a community. The students looked after each other. In the nine years I ran the scheme, we welcomed more than 90 students, with some staying five years. Many of the young people participated in the life of the church. We arranged for the older people to welcome them into their homes. They ran social events, such as a car trial, for the older people. A large group of the older people met every Monday night to play mahjong and welcomed some of the younger people. Good relationships were formed across the age divide. The congregation did not grow much beyond the older people and the young people who were living in its property. But it was well sustained over the years I was there.

After I left, the church began to struggle to find a continuing stream of young people to come into the community which we had formed. It also began to decline as older people passed away. Twenty-five years later, the remnant merged with another church and the property was sold. I know some of students who were present in that church continue to worship in other churches and a handful of people who were part of the church continue to be active in the congregation into which they were 'officially' merged.

Uniting Church in suburban Melbourne
sold and ready for the site to be re-purposed.

After concluding my time as a minister of congregations and moving full-time into research, I joined another church in the suburbs of Melbourne. It was a small and warm congregation with about 75 people in the church directory and an average attendance of about 45. We were there for about 8 years when the minister retired and the congregation grew anxious about finding and paying for another minister. They decided they needed to merge with another larger congregation. This occurred about 15 years ago. Of those 75 people in the first church, some have died, some decided not to go to church, and about 12 have some contact with the church into which we were merged. The church building which served us twenty-five years ago is now part of a mental health facility.

The patterns that I have observed throughout my life have certainly not been encouraging in terms of the vitality of church life or the size and number of churches. My experience has been that simply to maintain numbers has taken a lot of work and effort. In general, most of the older people have told me that their children are no longer involved, or certainly not on a regular basis. In most cases, as older people have died, they have not been replaced by younger people. Many churches are simply dying as the older generation passes away. In the suburb in which I now live, the Catholic, Anglican and Uniting churches have all closed. A Pentecostal church has started in a local high school, but is not large. An independent Baptist church is still functioning in the area.

These patterns of declining vitality and the closure of churches which I have experienced are common throughout Australia and through many other parts of the world. Analysis of data from censuses provides some numerical measures which parallel these trends.

The 2021 Census

The census is one of the major sources of information about the lives and culture of the population. Because everyone is required to complete the census form, it provides very detailed and accurate pictures. Every five years, people have been asked what is their religion. It is an optional question, but most people respond to it. In fact, in the last census in 2021, just 7 per cent of the population did not answer the question (which is noted as optional on the census form) or wrote in an answer that the Australian Bureau of Statistics could not classify. This proportion was down from

10 per cent who did not answer the question in 2016, which is comparable to previous censuses. In fact, nearly half of those who do not answer the question do not fill in a census form at all. Most of these people are on walk-about, sailing around the coast or are in inaccessible, locked inner-city residential apartments.

As shown in Figure 1, in 2021 just 44 per cent of the population identified as Christian or identified with a Christian denomination, down from 52 per cent in 2016, and 68 per cent in 2001. If we go back to 1921, 97 per cent of the population identified as Christian. Then it declined to 86 per cent from 1933 through to 1971. Since then, the proportion of Christians has been declining in each census, but more rapidly from 2011.

Figure 1. The Percentage of the Australian Population Identifying as Christian or with a Christian Denomination in the Censuses

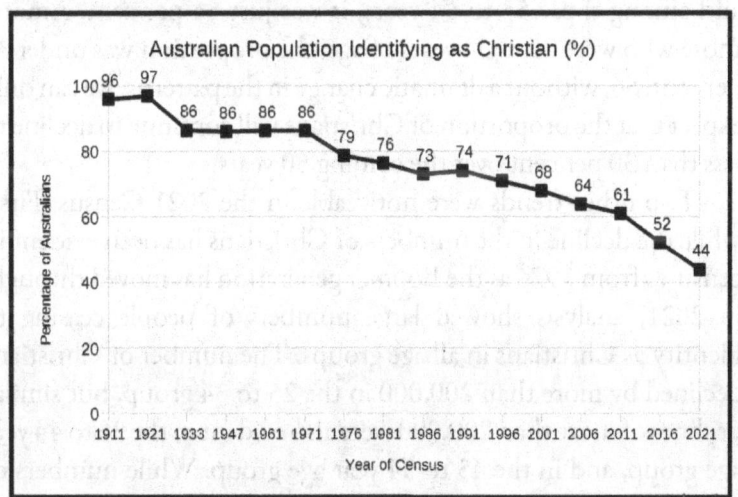

Source: Various Australian censuses

While the proportion of Christians has been declining, the actual numbers of Christians kept rising until 2011, due to the increasing number of people in the Australian population. But this changed in 2016, with the actual number of Christians declining, despite increases in the population and that trend continued in 2021. A total of just over 11 million Australians identified as Christian in 2021, about the same number of Christians as in 1981.

The decline began with from the Baby Boomer generation which we can define as those born between 1946 and 1964. It is just the head of the household who fills in the Census for everyone in the home. So it was in the 1970s that Boomers began setting up their own homes and filling in the Census for themselves. Large numbers of them began to describe themselves as having no religion. This set the scene for the gradual decline in the percentage of Christians in the Australian population. The Boomers are now retiring. In 2021, the oldest of them was 75 years old. Among those Australians 75 years and older, 69 per cent said they identified as Christian. Among those 65 to 74 years old, it was just 60 per cent, and among those 55 to 64 years, it was just 54 per cent. Among those who were 25 to 34 years of age, the proportion was under 30 per cent. So, without a dramatic change in the patterns, we can only expect that the proportion of Christians will continue to decline to less than 30 per cent over the coming 50 years.

Two other trends were noticeable in the 2021 Census. First, while the decline in the numbers of Christians has been evident in censuses from 1976 as the Boomer generation has moved through, in 2021, analysis showed large numbers of people ceasing to identify as Christians in all age groups. The number of Christians declined by more than 200,000 in the 25 to 34 group, but similar declines of more than 200,000 were also evident in the 35 to 44 year age group, and in the 45 to 54 year age group. While numbers of Christians went up a little in the 65 and older age group, they were not keeping up with the rapid increase of people in that age group. When compared with the increased numbers of people in that age group, it was evident that many older people were also ceasing to identify as Christian.

Second, in the comparison of past censuses, the numbers of Christians in the capital cities has fallen more rapidly than outside the capital cities. Thus, the Christian identity in rural and regional Australia has remained relatively strong. But in 2021 compared with 2011, the decline in rural areas was greater than in the capital cities. The rural areas still had a higher proportion identifying as Christian than the capital cities in most of the states, but the difference was slight throughout Australia and the rate of decline was much greater in the rural areas than in the capital cities in every state of Australia. For example, the number of Christians declined in rural Western Australia by 33 per cent in the decade from 2011 to 2021, compared with just 11 per cent in Perth. In New South Wales, the rural decline was 19 per cent compared with 10 per cent in Sydney.

It is also noteworthy that there has been a sharp decline among Aboriginal and Torres Strait Islander peoples in their identification as Christian. In 2011, 62 per cent identified as Christian. In 2021, just 41 per cent identified as Christian. There was a corresponding rise in the proportion saying they had no religion, from 24 per cent in 2011 to 51 per cent in 2021. There may be special reasons for this change in religious identity which are discussed in Chapter Two.

In summary, the overall picture from the censuses is that the decline in both the proportion and absolute numbers of Christians is accelerating through all age groups and in all parts of Australia, rural and urban, including indigenous people.

It should be noted that the decline is much greater in some denominations than in others. We will examine this in Chapter Six. We can also note at this point that immigration has had some impact on the figures. The increase in the numbers of Buddhists, Hindus, Muslims and Sikhs since the end of the White Australia Policy – which basically meant that Australia only accepted immigrants from Europe up to the 1970s – has had some impact. However, the increase in adherents of other religions through immigration does not offset the decrease in Christians. We will explore this in detail in Chapter Five.

Information from surveys

The census has just one question on religion: "What is your religion?" There are many reasons why people indicate that they are Christian. In 2011, a sociologist, Abby Day, published the results of a study she had conducted in the United Kingdom in which people were asked why they answered the question on the census the way they did. For some people, it was a matter of heritage - "We have always been Christian". Some would add, "Well, we are certainly not Hindu or Muslim, so we must be Christian". Others answered "Christian" because they had been involved in working for a Christian organisation. Some saw Christianity as basis of their morals, but certainly did not hold onto Christian beliefs. On the other hand, continued belief in God was a reason for others to describe themselves as Christian. It is likely Australians identify with a Christian denomination for a similar range of reasons.

While 11 million Australians still identified as Christian in 2021, only a small number were involved in Christian churches. The usual way we measure the numbers involved in a church is by counting the number who attend a church monthly or more often. It is not quite accurate as there are many devout people who simply cannot get to church, even monthly. It may be a matter of health or mobility. Or it may be because there is no church (or no church of their denomination) which is close enough to attend. But many people who describe themselves as Christian do not feel it is necessary to go frequently to a church. It is enough to go to church at Christmas and Easter or on special saints' days, or enough to live as a 'good person'.

Surveys can tell us much more than the census about people's religious practices. The *Australian Survey of Social Attitudes*

(AuSSA) is conducted annually by the Australian Consortium for Social and Political Research (ACSPRI) which is a non-profit organisation supported by many universities and government research agencies. It is used widely by government departments, universities and other organisations as a reliable source of information about Australians' social attitudes, beliefs and opinions. A component of this survey is the International Social Survey Project (ISSP), which means that it includes a selection of questions used in around 40 countries around the world. The ISSP component moves through a cycle of topics and has had a focus on religion approximately every nine years: in 1993, 2001, 2009, and 2018. While it is just a sample survey of between 1,200 and 2,500 people, it gives us some indication about religious practices and how they are changing. Table 1 presents some responses to questions about religion which have been asked over several years.

Table 1. Percentage of Australian Adults Responding to Various Questions on Religion 1993 to 2018

	1993	2001	2009	2018
Belief in God without doubts	34	30	26	25
Belief in higher being or believe sometimes	45	49	43	35
Don't know or don't believe in God	21	21	31	40
Don't believe in God but used to	22	32	39	48
Pray weekly or more often	38	29	21	19
Attend religious services monthly or more often	26	23	16	13
Attend Christian church monthly or more often	25.5	22	15	10.5

Source: *Australian Survey of Social Attitudes* in various years.

Table 1 shows that in every measure of Australian adults' beliefs and practices, there has been a significant decline between 1993 and 2018. The proportion of the population believing in God without doubts has dropped from one third (34%) to one quarter (25%), while the percentage who do not know whether it is possible to know whether God exists or do not believe in God has risen from 21 per cent to 40 per cent.

Increasingly, people have reported that they used to believe in God, but they do not believe now. In 2018, almost half the population reported that.

The proportion of the population who said they prayed weekly or more often has halved from 38 per cent to 19 per cent. And the proportion attending religious services has also halved, from 26 per cent 13 per cent. The proportion of the Australian population attending a Christian church has decreased a little more than that, down from almost 26 per cent to just 10.5 per cent in 2018.

There has never been a time in Australia when the majority of people went to church frequently. While there were no reliable surveys in early years, anecdotal evidence suggests that it may not have been much above one quarter of the population for most of the time that Europeans have been living in Australia. Church attendance possibly reached its maximum in the 1960s around the time of the Billy Graham Crusades in Australia. The first major survey of religion in Australia was conducted in 1966 by Hans Mol, Professor of Religious Studies at McMaster University, Canada and visiting Fellow at the Australian National University. He reported in his book *The Faith of Australians* (1985) that, according to the 1966 survey, 33 per cent of the adult population attended a church monthly or more often with little variation across the age groups.

Mol also reported that around half the population said they believed in God and had no doubts about it. However, there was some difference with age, older people being more certain of

God's existence than younger people. Around 30 per cent said they prayed daily, although the proportion varied from 22 per cent who were 20 to 24 years of age through to 46 per cent of those who were aged 60 years or older.

In that 1966 survey, the comparison of the different age groups suggests that the decline in religious belief and practice had already begun, with older people reporting higher levels of belief and practice than younger people. Belief and practice have certainly declined since that time.

It is sometimes suggested that the decline in religion in Australia is mostly among those who were nominally Christian while most of those who were actively and devotedly Christian have stayed true to their beliefs and practices. This fits a particular theological view which suggests that when a person is truly converted and committed, they retain that commitment. These people might argue that people who have left the faith were never truly Christian. They might have described themselves as Christian on a census, but they were never truly committed.

It is certainly true that many people who never attended church, but used to call themselves Christian on the census, now describe themselves as having 'no religion'. In the past, it was not exactly socially respectable to call oneself an atheist. It was as bad as calling oneself a communist! All good people were Christian! Since the 1970s, it has become increasingly acceptable to describe oneself as an atheist or as having no religion. Thus, it makes sense that people who were only Christian because of its social acceptability no longer feel they need to claim that.

However, the data from the *Australian Survey of Social Attitudes* show that many people who have been involved in the churches, have believed in God without doubt, and have prayed frequently, have decided they no longer believe and have ceased their practice of faith. That survey data indicates that more than 4 million Australian adults were attending a church at least monthly in 1993 whereas in 2018 it was less than 2 million. This change cannot be explained just by the death of older people or the departure of nominal Christians. People who were once involved in a church are now no longer involved. While many people who were nominally Christian are no longer Christian, that also applies to people who were committed to their faith.

Other religions

How does this fit with the growth that is being experienced in some other religions in Australia? As shown in Table 2, the fastest growing religion in Australia between 2011 and 2021 was Sikhism, growing by 191 per cent in that decade. Sikhism is the religion of many of the people living in the Punjab region of India. The Sikhs separated themselves from the Hindus and the Muslims in a similar period to the Protestant Reformation in Europe. The percentage of those in the 25 to 34 age group identifying with each religious group is also provided in Table 2. This gives a very rough idea of the potential proportion of the population (without taking into account future immigration or differences in birthrates in the different religious groups) in five or six decades to come.

Table 2. Religious Identity among Australians in 2011 and 2021

Religious Identity	2011 Numbers	2021 Numbers	Change (%)	2011 (% of population)	2021 (% of population)	Percent of all 25 to 34 years old
Buddhist	528,997	615,823	16.4	2.5	2.4	2.9
Christian	13,150,671	11,148,814	-15.2	61.1	43.9	28.9
Hindu	275,534	684,002	148.2	1.3	2.7	4.8
Islam	476,291	813,392	70.8	2.2	3.2	4.2
Jewish	97,335	99,956	2.7	0.5	0.4	0.3
Sikh	72,296	210,400	191.0	0.3	0.8	1.8
No religion	4,796,786	9,840,996	105.1	22.3	38.7	48.4
Population	21,507,716	25,422,788	18.2	100.0	100.0	100.0

Source: Australian Bureau of Statistics, National Population Censuses 2011 and 2021.

Hinduism, the religion of the majority of Indians, is also growing very rapidly in Australia, with growth of 148 per cent between 2011 and 2021. Islam is growing less rapidly than Hinduism, but grew by 71 per cent in that same decade. Buddhists grew by 16 per cent in the decade while the number of Christians declined by 15 per cent.

Does the growth in these other religions mean that it is just Christianity experiencing decline? How can we really talk about secularisation if other religions are experiencing significant growth? And news reports suggest that there is growth in other religions overseas. We hear of growth in the devotion and activities of Muslims, Hindus and other groups in many places.

The growth in other religions in Australia has occurred very largely through immigration. There have been few Australians of European descent who have become Buddhists, Hindus or Muslims. The most popular religion, other than Christianity, among Australians of European ancestry has been Buddhism. The 2021 Census found that of all Buddhists in Australia, 17 per cent said they were of Australian or European ancestry. Most Buddhists came from Asia.

In 2021, of all those who described themselves as Buddhist, 24 per cent were born in Australia. Of Sikhs, it was 25 per cent. Of Hindus, it was 20 per cent. Almost all the growth has come from immigrants coming to Australia from various parts of Asia. Most migrants come in their 20s. Some are married and others are single. In their late 20s, they begin having children, usually in Australia. Thus the majority of those people who identify with these other religions who were born in Australia are the children of immigrants. The proportion born in Australia does not represent converts, but rather the children born into immigrant families. They want their children to keep their language, culture and values too. Involvement with their religious communities helps them to bring up their children within their own culture.

Large numbers of Muslims started arriving in Australia from Lebanon following the war there in 1969. So some Muslims have been in Australia for several generations. Other Muslims have joined them from various parts of the Middle East, from Africa and Asia. More than most other groups, they have emphasised their distinctiveness, and worked hard to maintain their communities, their languages, their customs and values. Religious faith has been a significant part of that process. Thus, nearly 40 per cent of Muslims indicated in the 2021 Census that they had been born in Australia. It is likely that some of these people are second or third generation Australians.

However, the Australian Bureau of Statistics has released some longitudinal data, which allows us to trace how people have identified themselves in the 2006, 2011 and 2016 censuses. These data show that there have been people from religions other than Christianity who have begun describing themselves as having no religion. As yet, the numbers are relatively small because so many of the people associated with these religions have arrived in Australia recently. Table 3 shows the percentages who moved into the religion and the percentage who moved out into no religion between 2006 and 2011.

Table 3. Proportion of People Identifying with Various Religions Moving into No Religion between 2006 and 2016

Religious Group	Moved into No Religion between 2006 and 2016 (% of those identifying in 2006)	Moved from No Religion into the Group between 2006 and 2016 (% of those identifying in 2016)	Number of people moving into no religion
Buddhism	23.3	1.59	97,750
Christianity	16.6	6.8	1,987,709
Hinduism	5.44	0.24	8058
Islam	7.61	0.27	25,903
Judaism	11.21	0.11	9,958
Sikhism	4.24	0.04	1,121

Source: ABS Longitudinal Data

Table 3 shows that close to 100,000 Buddhists moved into no religion over the decade. Almost 26,000 Muslims also moved, as did smaller numbers of Hindus, Jews and Sikhs. The general pattern is that, the longer immigrants live in Australia, the more likely they adopt the major patterns of the Australian culture. It is highly likely that people will continue to move from each of these other religions into no religion in the second, third and subsequent generations. The pattern of secularisation currently having a major impact on Christianity is likely to have an increasing effect on these other religions over time.

International trends

For years, prominent American sociologists, such as Rodney Stark, argued that secularisation was not occurring and the United States was evidence of that. However, in 2023, three American sociologists, Isabella Kasselstrand, Phil Zuckerman and Ryan Craygun published a book, *Beyond Doubt: The Secularisation of Society* which clearly refuted Rodney Stark and his collaborators. They analysed data from around the world, arguing that almost every country was showing signs of secularisation, including the United States of America.

They argued that secularisation tends to occur in three stages: behaviour, belonging and finally belief. The first sign of secularisation is that people no longer attend religious services as frequently. David Voas, another well-known scholar in the sociology of religion who has studied the international data, has argued this behaviour change often occurs over generations. Thus, the children of those who attended church no longer do so when they make their own decisions about it. According to the American sociologists, the second stage is that people cease to have a sense of belonging, or cease to identify. The third stage is that the residues of belief fade away. At the moment, a large proportion of the world's population believe in God or in gods, but there is evidence that these beliefs are fading.

The starting point, therefore, is to examine behaviour: in particular, attendance at religious services. Kasselstrand, Zuckerman and Craygun found the evidence in the World Values Surveys. However, the International Social Survey Data also provides evidence of declining attendance at religious services in a range of countries for various years as shown in Table 4.

Table 4. Attendance at Religious Services Monthly or More Often by Year for Various Countries (Percentages of Adults Attending)

Country	2001	2007	2018
Austria		29	21
Australia	22	19	13
Bulgaria		21	9
Chile		37	25
Taiwan		14	17
Croatia		42	35
Czech Republic		10	10
Finland		9	7
France		10	8
Germany	15	18	14
Hungary	25	14	15
Israel	55	26	25
Japan		10	5
Korea (South		33	29
New Zealand	22	17	18
Norway	11	13	8
Philippines	87	87	79
Russia	1	9	12
Slovak Republic		41	35
Slovenia		28	21
South Africa		83	43
Sweden		7	6
Switzerland		22	12
United Kingdom	22	21	19
USA	51	51	44

Sources: Datasets ZA2150, ZA5512, and ZA7570 from the International Social Survey Program. (Blank cells mean that the country did not participate in the survey that year.)

It should be noted that the data vary a little in quality from one country to another. Sample sizes and the ways the sample was achieved vary. The countries participating in any particular year also varied. However, there are some clear trends. In almost every case, there has been a decline in attendance in religious services in recent years. There are just two exceptions in the data above: Russia and Taiwan. In both cases, it has been suggested that the political contexts have changed, leading to increased involvement in religion. In the case of Russia, Putin's endorsement of and support for the Russian Orthodox Church has had an impact. In Taiwan, there is an increased sense of distinctiveness in relation to mainland China. In general, those countries which have moved out of communism when religious involvement was suppressed have seen a rise in involvement in religion. However, Kasselstrand, Zuckerman and Craygun, amongst other scholars, have argued that it is likely that the increase in involvement in these countries will only be temporary.

Unfortunately, we have almost no survey data from the world's two largest countries by population: China and India. In both cases, it is impossible to get accurate data on what is occurring. Recent reports from China suggest there has been an increase in the suppression of religion, leading to a decline in involvement. How long that suppression may last, and whether there will be something of a revival when suppression is lifted, cannot be predicted. The situation in India is also unknown. Politically, there has been a rise in Hindu nationalism. Whether that has led to a rise in involvement in religious practices is not known.

There are little reliable data from African countries. Again, the conflicts there may well have led to an increase in religious involvements. Kasselstrand, Zuckerman and Craygun report that Africa is the most religious continent in the world. However, they indicate there are signs religious attendance has begun to wane in some parts of Africa.

In summary

Personal experiences of declining attendances are backed up by census and survey data. The Australian censuses show both the percentage and numbers of people identifying as Christian is in decline in all parts of Australia and across all age groups. The survey data shows that the percentage of Australians attending church and believing in God has declined over recent decades. These trends are not unique to Australia. There is evidence of falling church attendances in most countries across the world.

There are theoretical reasons for expecting that these trends of declining belief, practice and identification will occur at different times in history and at different rates in different nations. It is expected that there will be some variability over time. There may be events and historical circumstances which lead to an increase in religious involvement for a time. But the general theory of secularisation suggests that the overall trend will be towards more secular societies across the world, following the observed trend in Australia. The following chapter will examine what is driving these changes.

Chapter 2

Understanding the Trends

Secularisation

We have observed in chapter one that there is a general decline in the proportion of Australians identifying with a religion, and particularly with Christianity. We have also noted that there is evidence from surveys of a decline in the proportions of Australians attending religious services, engaging in prayer and believing in God. These trends are part of the same social process that is generally referred to as secularisation.

'Secularisation' means more than people not being involved in religion as much as in the past. It also encompasses the removal of religion from the public sphere. It is visible in Australia when Christmas festivities – including public carol services – make little or no reference to the religious traditions which initiated them. Commemorations of those who have died in war – such as the services on ANZAC Day when Australians remember their own and New Zealand troops – used to be led by a minister of religion, but that is rarely the case today. In many places, public prayers at the start of meetings of the various levels of government have been replaced by a moment of reflection and an acknowledgment of indigenous custodians ... or nothing at all.

More important than the symbolic involvement of ministers or priests in public events is that there is little talk in the public sphere about God or about religious traditions. Few politicians in Australia make reference to God when talking about their policies, although they may refer to God in reference to their personal lives. It is now rare for a newspaper article to be written about the Christian faith, except about its demise, or about sexual abuse in religious institutions. I remember when most newspapers had someone who was tasked with covering religion in Australia. Those journalists used to phone me in my office at the Christian Research Association and ask if I had anything they could write about! That stopped happening about twenty years ago.

The public service operates largely without reference to religion. While religious communities operate some hospitals and aged care facilities, and many welfare programs, they are generally treated in a way similar to those which are operated by non-religious entities. They are held accountable for the spending of the public money which is given for their operation and are regulated in a similar way to other organisations.

Schools are a little different with close to 40 per cent of all students spending at least some of their schooling in a church-run school. Their size in the education system gives them some leverage to vary their educational practice compared to government-run schools, particularly in relation to religion. However, schools have to meet similar educational standards whatever their foundation.

Differentiation

The Belgian sociologist Karel Dobbelaere has long argued that secularisation is primarily a process in which different parts of modern societies become differentiated from each other, thus reducing the overarching role that religion once had. In their book, *Beyond Doubt: The Secularisation of Society*, Kasselstrand, Zuckerman, and Cragun argue that this process of 'differentiation' is the major driver of secularisation. Over time, distinct fields of knowledge have developed, each with their own experts. In the process, religion has ceased to be part of that field of knowledge. In themselves, these distinct fields of knowledge were not anti-religious. Rather, religion was simply not included in that field or that way of looking at things.

One of the first fields of knowledge to be developed in this way was astronomy. For millennia, people have looked at the stars and have tried to work out what the universe was really like. Some saw it as a great dome with one large light, the sun, which travelled across the dome each day, and with smaller lights such as the moon and the stars which also moved in various patterns across the sky. Some thought that heaven, where God the Creator dwelt, was beyond the dome of the stars.

Very few people challenged the idea that the earth was at the centre of the universe, around which the other elements circled. Some who made measurements were fascinated by the rather peculiar movements of the stars over the year. People such as the Greek astronomer Ptolemy developed quite complex ideas about how the movements of the stars might be explained.

The development of the telescope changed everything. In 1609, Galileo began examining the sky with a telescope and found that there were moons orbiting around other planets. His measurements with the telescope confirmed the theory of Copernicus and other astronomers that, in fact, the earth moved around the sun. The earth was not the centre of the universe.

Religious authorities vigorously opposed Galileo. The Bible says that "the sun went down". So it must be the sun that moves and not the earth. The Bible was the supreme authority. The astronomers must be wrong. But as more people looked at the skies, they found that the astronomers were correct. Their description of how the earth moved around the sun actually made much more sense than the complex account of the movements of the heavenly bodies provided by Ptolemy. Galileo never directly challenged the existence of God or of the heavens. But he had introduced a different authority, based on careful observations and measurements, which meant that, at least in this area of thinking, neither the church nor the Bible were the supreme authorities.

Over the following centuries, scientific ways of thinking developed. People like Isaac Newton, who was as much a theologian as a scientist, began to explain the world in terms of natural laws. He explained regularities which could easily be observed in terms of simple principles. The falling of an apple from a tree could be explained by the same principle as the movement of the tides. It was all a matter of gravity. The power to explain the world that Isaac Newton offered caught the imagination of ordinary people. Here was a new way of making sense of so much that was happening around them. Isaac Newton was not intending his laws as a replacement for God, but reference to God was no longer necessary to explain the movement of the tides or the falling of apples from trees.

Another significant development in thinking came from the pen of Charles Darwin. He propounded the theory that species of plants and animals have evolved from earlier forms through impersonal processes of natural selection. This was connected with the growing evidence from fossils and from other sources that the earth is much older than 6,000 years as had been calculated from the Biblical references to creation. The idea that God had not created the total variety of creatures that existed in one creative day – as suggested in the first chapter of the Bible – was revolutionary to many people. But the new way of seeing the world made a great deal of sense as people examined the huge variety of species of plants and animals that existed and how they might have evolved differently in different environments. Again, the world was being explained without reference to religion and in ways that contradicted some of the ideas that had their roots in religious traditions.

The statue of Charles Darwin in the Natural History Museum, London. Darwin provided an alternative way of explaining the existence of the great variety of species of plants and animals through his theory of evolution.

In the late 18th century and through the 19th and 20th centuries, scientific thinking developed in many other spheres of knowledge including psychology, education, economics and agriculture. In many instances, the new ideas took the place of ideas which had their roots in religious traditions. For example, the work of Freud in suggesting that dreams might be explained by the working of the unconscious mind, rather than the result of supernatural messengers, was revolutionary. Dreams were no longer seen as the messages of angels or the work of demonic powers. They had a basis in the human mind that needed no reference to the supernatural.

Karl Marx not only provided theories about how society and the economy worked but raised questions about whether religion was, in fact, a good thing. He suggested that religion consisted of a set of ideas which powerful people used to keep control of others: the poor, slaves, and even employees. Religions, Marx argued, had maintained that if you do your duty to your employer or your master, you will be rewarded in heaven when you die. Marx said this was really a ruse to prevent the poor from rising up and claiming appropriate payment for what they had contributed to production. Marx famously said that religion was the opiate of the masses. It kept people drugged, giving them a false sense that there would be justice in the end. Justice would only come, said Marx, if there was a revolution in which the workers took control of the means of production and received due reward for their work.

This movement of differentiation, in which we understand the various aspects of life without reference to God, has continued. There was a time when farmers felt that prayer was most effective in ensuring that there was a good harvest. God would send the rain and ensure that the sun shone and produced good crops. Even in my youth, harvest festivals were major events in the churches, when we thanked God for the growth of our food. But over time, we have come to realise that soil fertility, careful irrigation, the management of weeds, and other processes were all more important in ensuring there was a good crop. So the idea of praying for a good harvest has faded. It was never seen as wrong, just no longer necessary.

It also used to be common to pray for people who were travelling. Indeed, in the past, travel was often dangerous. No one could be sure what would happen on the journey. There could be bandits beside the roads or pirates on the seas. Ships could be sunk is storms. Carriages could get caught by floods. Travelling outside one's own country could be particularly dangerous. There are still places in the world where travel is dangerous and it is not uncommon for there to be religious rituals for those who are travelling. I was recently in Thailand where such rituals are common amongst the Buddhist population, and comparable prayers in the Thai Christian community are widespread.

Yet, most Westerners rely mostly on having their cars serviced, on having well-kept roads and appropriate detours if there are floods. If travelling by plane, we consider it highly important that the airline industry is well regulated, and that the servicing of the planes is maintained at the highest level. We do not expect anything to go wrong. For most people, the need for prayer when we travel has faded. We rely more on the science and engineering underpinning our means of travel, the high-quality construction of our cars, trains, ships and planes, and the high level of regulation of travel industries. The place of religion in making travel safe has largely disappeared.

Perhaps one of the last areas in which prayer has continued to play a role has been in relation to human health. There were times when prayer was one of the few options people had when they were sick. Today, most Australians, like most people of nations with modern medical services, turn to doctors and the health system to deal with illness. It is widely accepted that many illnesses are caused by bacteria and viruses, and other health problems are due to weaknesses in our human structure. Many of the problems can be rectified by medicine, surgery and other forms of treatment. Most Australians would not think of seeking additional assistance from God.

At the same time, many people do pray in times of sickness. Some illnesses are not curable. Hence, people turn to whatever measures might work. They turn to herbal or other non-conventional medicines, and some also turn to prayer. Prayer costs little, and there is always the chance it could have a positive effect.

Nevertheless, for most, the body is understood in terms of health and medical science and the major practitioners are those who have had the appropriate scientific training.

None of these areas of thought – astronomy, evolution, agricultural science, or medical science – require us to give up belief in God. Rather, they simply do not need to include reference to God. Accordingly, many Australians live their lives with no reference to God and without seeing the need for prayer. The idea of God is not rejected. Rather the idea of God has faded into irrelevance for many Australians.

On the other hand, perhaps half of the Australian population continue to believe there is a God. How could there be a universe without some great force which brought it into existence? How can we explain why the universe operates in very regular ways which can be explained by natural laws if there was no 'intelligent' being who created the universe? These believers feel that God is present in the beauty of the universe, in the intricacy, complexity and interdependence of the natural world.

Many people believe that personal 'coincidences' are evidence that God is involved in their lives. They point to many instances where prayers have seemingly been answered. They constantly pray to God and feel they are sharing their lives with God. While the place of religion in the thinking and in the behaviour of most people has greatly reduced over the last century, religion is far from fading out of Australian society altogether. As noted in chapter one, more than half of all Australians believe in God or a higher being, and half continue to identify with one religious group or another, a total of 13 per cent attend religious services and a higher proportion of Australians engage in some forms of religious rituals.

The overall result has been that scientific ways of thinking have come to form the basis of the common formal body of knowledge that we impart through education. It has come to provide the basic assumptions which provides the ground for our communication. No one knows all of science, but we know that within science there is knowledge about how things work. For example, there are many medical specialists who have knowledge about how particular parts of the body work but no one with all the expertise. So we turn to them for advice when the body is not operating as we think it should.

There is one area which remains important for religion: that of values. It is frequently said by people committed to the Christian faith that without religion there will be a moral vacuum. This will be the topic of the next chapter. First, however, we will note some other factors which contribute to secularisation.

Identity

In the 1970s, David Martin, a prominent English sociologist and Anglican priest, undertook a study of the world-wide patterns of religious identity and attendance at religious services. In *A General Theory of Secularization*, he noted how the rates of attendance varied greatly from one place to another. At that time, religious identity and attendance were much higher in places like Ireland and South Korea, and some countries in Africa. There have been higher levels of religiosity in the Middle East, including Iran and Afghanistan, than in most of the Western world.

Martin suggested that these high levels of religiosity often had to do with the national identity of those countries: how they saw themselves in relation to the countries around them, or even in relation to the rest of the world. Many countries contrast themselves with neighbouring countries, emphasising their distinctive characteristics. Thus, Ireland has long contrasted itself with England. It took centuries to shed itself of British domination, and the spectre of the more powerful England has long overshadowed the country. Part of the Irish identity has been its Catholicism which it has contrasted with the dominance of Protestantism in England. Martin has suggested that this contributed to the previous high levels of identifying as Catholic in Ireland and correspondingly high levels of religious involvement.

A similar claim has been made in relation to South Korea which has defined itself over against North Korea. Not only has South Korea identified itself through its capitalist economy compared with the authoritarian communist regime, but also through its religiosity, both Christian and Buddhist, as against the atheism of the north.

One of the few countries in which religious leaders currently provide senior roles in government, Iran has had a chequered history, particularly through the 20th century. The oil interests of the USA and Britain and their desire to stop Iran supporting Germany in the World Wars led to many controls being placed on the Shah and the government. Within this context, many aspects of Iranian heritage and Islamic culture were suppressed. Reza Shah ruled from 1926 to 1941 and tried to Westernise Iran. He enforced European dress and in 1936 the wearing of the hijab was banned. He required that chairs be used in mosques. The authoritarian Westernisation of Iran led to great unrest and uprisings in which many were killed and injured. The involvement of the USA in Iranian politics continued after World War II largely because of their oil industry interests, which the Iranian parliament had voted to nationalise. The USA supported a military coup which removed the prime minister. Thus, when the Islamic Revolution finally removed the Shah and changed the structure of the government in 1979, the Western powers, and USA in particular, were seen as the great enemy of the people. Islam was strongly endorsed as central to Iran's identity, in contrast with the Christianity of the Western world.

The influence of Iran and Saudi Arabia in the Middle East and in parts of Africa has contributed to the rise of Islamic identity in other countries. It has also strengthened the sense that Islam is antagonistic to the Western world. In some ways, it prepared the soil for the terrorist attacks in the Western world that took place early in the 21st century, which, in turn, have led to some people in the Western world demonising Islam and Iran in particular. As some Islamic countries have strengthened their sense of identity in relation to the West through their adherence to Islam, so the national identity has contributed to the high levels of religious identity and involvement in those nations.

As tensions between the Western world and Islamic countries have eased in some places such as Indonesia, so the importance of Islam as a distinguishing feature of those countries has weakened. The war between Hamas and Israel, however, has renewed and increased the tensions, and again the distinction between the Islamic world and the Western world has been heightened. The war in Gaza has had some impact on the sense of religious identity in Australia. It has led to a strengthening of the sense of identity with Gaza among Palestinian and other Islamic immigrants and to a widespread condemnation of Israel and its Jewish Zionist identity.

The site of the Dome of the Rock is sacred to Jews, Christians and Muslims. The tensions over control over the area arises out of the mix of ethnic and religious identity.

In turn, Israel is one country in which over recent decades there has been an increase in the levels of religiosity. The levels of tension between Israel and its neighbours has contributed to the strength of its Jewish heritage and character. In an international study I conducted in 2013, reported in an article in the *Journal of Implicit Religion*, 'Spirituality and Religious Tolerance', Israel was the one country in 40 measured in the International Social Survey program in 2008 in which more young people than older people identified themselves as spiritual and/or religious.

There is another example of identity politics influencing religious identity within Australia. Over recent years, there has been a rise in the identity and pride of First Nations peoples. The sense that they have the world's longest continuing culture over perhaps 65,000 years has been reinforced in many contexts. The fact that they were brutally pushed out of the lands in which they have lived for thousands of years by the British colonialists has been widely recognised. The Federal government has admitted its wrongdoing in removing many thousands of Aboriginal children from their families in order to 'Westernise' them. As a result of these changes in attitude, people who had part Aboriginal heritage have recognised that side of their identity. Thus, there has been a dramatic rise in the proportion of the population indicating on the census that they had Aboriginal or Torres Strait Islander heritage from 2.6 per cent to 3.2 per cent between 2011 and 2021 while the proportion identifying as having no religion rose from 24 to 51 per cent. It seems very likely that this change in identity and the rise in the distinctiveness of the Aboriginal and Torres Strait Islander culture and heritage has also contributed to the rejection of the Christian identity that many of them previously held. Christianity has been seen by some First Nations people as part of the colonial identity which was foisted upon them. They see the churches as being complicit in the removal of children from family, the Stolen

Generation, so many First Nations people have come to reject the Christian faith.

Denominational identity

While national and ethnic identities can have an impact on religious identity and thus can contribute to or resist the forces of secularisation, so the issues of identity can also have an impact within a local community. I remember meeting with a couple who lived in a caravan park with their two children. They had had issues of drug and alcohol dependence and had very little income. I invited them to come to church, but they were very reluctant. They did not have the right clothes to wear to church. They did not have proper shoes but lived in their sandals. They did not use the same vocabulary. They simply felt that they would not fit in.

Different denominations have catered for different groups in Australian society. For many of the Protestant churches, one needed to be able to read well to participate in the responsive prayers and liturgy, or to maintain the personal Bible reading that was expected of members.

With the expectation in many Baptist churches, for example, that members abstained from alcoholic drinks altogether, it would be very hard for someone who drank regularly to fit in, let alone if one was addicted to alcohol. The Baptists have expected their members to take an active part in making decisions with the whole community as to how the church should run. It has tended to attract those who are relatively well educated.

While sermons in Baptist churches tend to be practical and oriented towards how one should live, sermons in Uniting Churches tend to be more philosophical or theological. There is a tendency for Uniting Church ministers to explore theoretical and academic issues, whether they are explaining passages in the Bible or contemplating aspects of life and society. Uniting Churches have appealed to a different group of people – often people with high levels of formal education who enjoyed abstract thinking.

The Salvation Army has been better than most denominations at welcoming those who had little education and who had addictions. It was formed to work amongst the poorest in the slums around London and has continued the tradition of seeking to help the poorest people in the society. In such ways, denominations have developed identities in which one group has felt included and others have felt excluded.

Over time, in Australia it has been the more educated and those of higher class who have attended church. Past census analysis has shown that in the poorer parts of the major cities, a high proportion of the population identify as Christian, but comparatively few attend the churches. They have generally felt that they were not able to identify with those who did attend, that they lacked the education and the skills of those who attended. Sometimes, it was just that people did not enjoy the sort of music used in churches.

The appeal of churches to those with a particular level and type of education has not been so apparent in the Catholic churches. With the focus on the ritual of the Mass, all that was required of those who attended was the simple ritual of going to the altar to receive the communion wafer. While there would be a short homily, there was not the expectation that was present in Protestant churches that people would read the Bible for themselves or that they would be involved in Bible studies. Most of the responses of the people within the service were learnt by heart. Thus, Catholic churches contain a greater variety of people across the socio-economic spectrum than Protestant denominations.

Throughout Australian society, Catholic and Protestant identities were reinforced by their mutual opposition to each other. It was apparent as far back as the 1788 first fleet of convicts from Britain when the British government sent a Protestant clergyman to conduct Christian services. The first church built in Australia was burnt down by Catholic convicts as a protest about the requirement to attend Protestant church services. Eventually, in 1820, the British government permitted the Catholic Church to send two priests. But the sectarian divisions have continued both at social level and at personal levels. It has only been in the past generation that Catholics and Protestants have felt they could attend each other's weddings and funerals and worship together for special occasions. To some extent, the sectarianism represented the conflict between the English and the Irish, but it had the effect of reinforcing religious identity on both sides.

Thus, national, racial and class identity can strengthen and weaken religious identity in different contexts. If there is an overall decline in racism and in wars across nations and struggles between different groups within nations, then it is likely that there will be a general decline in religious identity. For example, it seems is likely that the decline in tensions between England and Ireland contributed to the recent decline in religious involvement in Ireland.

In summary

Secularisation is often linked to modernisation. Modernisation can be thought of as a movement in which technology and ways of operating based on scientific thinking and on abstract technical bureaucracies are taking over. Differentiation is one of the processes within modernisation which has led to the adoption of scientific ways of thinking in various areas of knowledge. It is the differentiation aspect of modernisation which is one of the major drivers of secularisation. As scientific thinking and associated technological methods have been developed in the different areas of society, so religious thinking in those areas was no longer needed.

In astronomy, physics, geology and biology, for example, scientific thinking has developed in which there was no place for God. Belief in God was not explicitly rejected but was no longer needed.

As modern patterns of thinking developed in sociology and psychology, there were some attempts to explain religious thinking. It was seen as a product of social class divisions by Marx, for example, or as an infantile need for a father figure by Freud. While these explanations have not been widely accepted, the critique of religion itself had begun. More importantly, however, the development of thinking in sociology and psychology proceeded without reference to the input of God or gods.

Gradually, people have turned less to religion as a way of dealing with life. Prayer was no longer seen as necessary for a good harvest. Nor was prayer necessary for safe travel, or for healing sickness.

In some places, religious identity has been maintained because of its links with national or regional identity. It was a factor in the tensions between Iran and the Western world, particularly the United States. It is still a factor in wars and in civil conflicts, such as in the war between Hamas and Israel. But as conflicts are resolved, so religious identity may weaken.

The factors which have been discussed in this chapter mostly relate to changes in thinking and practice which have occurred over the last couple of centuries. They relate to the fading of religion in scientific thinking and in everyday life. The issues of national identity explain why nations may have higher or lower rates of involvement at particular times in history. At the level of the individual and socio-economic groups, identity also explains the involvement in churches of some people and the sense of exclusion among others. However, none of these factors explain the sharp down-turn in religious practice and belief that has been experienced in Australia in the last fifty years.

The missing driver of these recent trends has to do with values. The following chapter will examine how changes in values are affecting religious beliefs and practice, and explore the factors driving these changes in values.

Chapter 3

The Change in Personal Values

From duty to family life to personal fulfilment

One area of thinking which has continued to be influenced by religion is that of moral values. When Britain first sent its convicts to Australia, it also sent chaplains to have a moral influence on the convicts and, hopefully, change their ways. Since that time, many Australians have looked to religion for moral guidance, or justified their moral values by reference to religion. Some Australians are concerned that the fading of religion is contributing to a downward spiral in moral behaviour.

A particular focus has been family life. In various ways, churches have promoted the value of family life. Through the ceremony of marriage, churches have proclaimed that the union of men and women in marriage is holy, reflecting the union of Christ and the church. Through baptism or christening of children or through dedication in some Protestant churches, it is announced that each child is precious and is part of the family of God. Through the provision of educational institutions, both day schools and Sunday schools, churches have participated in the rearing of children. Most denominations have encouraged their members to marry and have children. The Catholic Church still forbids the use of artificial methods of contraception, even for married couples.

Churches have also discouraged, and sometimes totally condemned, behaviour which threatened family structures and which do not lead to having children. For example, they have discouraged divorce. Some churches do not allow divorced people to participate in certain rituals, or to re-marry in the church. Most churches have vigorously opposed homosexuality, and when the possibility of legalising same-sex marriage was debated in Australia, almost all Christian denominations opposed it.

Many denominations have been vigorously opposed to abortion. The Catholic Church in particular has been strident in its opposition. Abortions have been banned at Catholic hospitals, sometimes even when the life of the mother was endangered. They have argued that every foetus should be treated with respect due to every human person and hence abortion is the deliberate killing of an innocent person.

By the 1970s, the belief of many Christians that the focus for women's lives should be bearing and raising children had become very contentious. Prior to that time, men were commonly seen as having a leadership role, making the final decision in the home as well as in society, and providing the economic basis for the home. This was reinforced by the fact that only men were allowed to lead – to be priests or ministers – in the churches of many denominations. Thus in both church and home, women were expected to take subservient roles with a focus on caring for their children and their husbands..

Since the 1970s, with reliable methods of birth control, and much assistance in the home from new forms of technology, many women have found great fulfilment in their careers and in other contributions to the wider community. Many women first began to experience this during World War II when they took the place in the workplace and community of men who were overseas fighting in the war. After the war, the women went back to their homes as men returned to the workplace. However, it was not long before women began seeking greater opportunities for their abilities. The feminist movement arose in the 1960s and 1970s, calling for equality in all areas of life and society for males and females. Females could lead and should lead in government and business equally with men. The feminist movement rejected the subservience that many Christian churches and other religious groups expected of women.

The feminist movement supported the right to abortion. Abortion was seen as one of the ways in which women could maintain control over their bodies and over their lives. If they did not want a child, for health, economic or other reasons, women should not be compelled to proceed with a pregnancy, they said..

Thus, particularly since the 1970s, some aspects of what has traditionally been seen as Christian morality, particularly in relation to family life, have been widely questioned in Australia and other Western societies.

The prominent American sociologist, Ronald Inglehart, who is well known for his work on global changes in values, has put this into a broader perspective in his book *Religion's sudden decline: what's causing it, and what comes next?* He has argued that for most of human history, the survival of societies has been dependent on the society having many children. Frequently, children died in childhood. They did not live to the age when they had children themselves. Hence, having many children, with the expectation that at least some would survive, was vital to the survival of society as a whole.

Throughout human history, there have been waves of plagues and other diseases which have killed large sectors of the society. In many parts of Europe, for example, plagues would wipe out up to half the population. Even as late as 1918, the Spanish flu killed perhaps 50 million people, more than all those who had died in World War I. Thus, having many children was fundamental for societies to maintain their numbers, let alone grow them. So the moral rules that encouraged women to focus on child-bearing and child-raising were considered foundational for society. Behaviour which was seen as threatening that role of child-bearing was condemned, including homosexual behaviour and abortion.

The advances in medical science in the 20th century, which saw child mortality rates diminish significantly and more control over plagues and pandemics, made it possible for the moral rules to change. In the latter part of the 20th century, it was no longer necessary for all women to focus on child-bearing in those parts of the world with a well-resourced, scientifically-based health care system.

Another dimension of family life, apart from the raising of children, is the care of the elderly and of those with a disability. For most of human history, that responsibility has fallen on the younger members of the family and mostly on women. Indeed, life has often been very difficult for older people who did not have family members to care for them. That duty of care was reinforced by religious faith and supported by religious communities.

The other advance in the 20th century in some Western countries, alongside the development of medical care, was the development of welfare systems. These systems have provided some alternative protection for the vulnerable, offering care to those with disability and to the aged. While most people continue to value the care that the family offers, there are now some options provided by the state, charitable organisations and by corporations. When the family is unable to provide the care that is needed, in many Western countries, external assistance may be available.

Australian Services Building (Centrelink) is the contact point between people and the welfare system. The system contributes to a sense of security for people and means that people are less dependent on their families. Thus the dependence on religion to reinforce the moral imperatives around family care have become less critical for wellbeing.

Inglehart has argued that the development of welfare systems has been a major driver in the process of secularisation. He held that the development of welfare systems has given many people in the nations in which those systems have been developed and are working well a sense of existential security. People have a sense that if something goes wrong, there are some safety nets, some additional resources and help. The family is not as necessary as it once was, and there is less dependence on those influences such as religion which reinforced the duties of the family in care.

Inglehart pointed to the fact that some of the world's lowest rates of religious attendance are in the Scandinavian countries, Norway, Sweden, Denmark and Finland, which have the strongest welfare systems. In contrast, the USA, which is highly developed scientifically and technologically, has a weak welfare system. Inglehart argued that this was one of the reasons why church involvement has been much higher in the USA than in Europe. In recent years, however, church involvement in the USA has declined significantly and sociologists now recognise that secularisation is also occurring there.

The lack of welfare systems in many parts of the world has been a reason for the continued vitality of religion. Religion has continued to provide reinforcement for family responsibilities to ensure that children and the elderly are cared for. At the same time, where there are few resources for care readily available in the wider community, religious organisations themselves have offered caring community. Thus, the practical impact of religious communities in promoting family duties has been important alongside the belief that God cares and that people can turn to God when in need. It is noteworthy that religious commitment is strongest in the poorest countries where there are few resources and where there is nothing by way of a welfare system. Countries like Afghanistan, Yemen and Somalia stand out as the most conservatively and intensely religious, but with great poverty, high child mortality rates, and little by way of modern medical resources or welfare systems.

Inglehart has argued that while societies, families and individuals have valued the duties to the family and to the wider community imposed by religion, it has come at considerable cost. For women, the costs have been very high in that they have often been restricted to the home, unable to use their abilities and capacities for their own fulfilment as well as for the benefit of the wider community. It has come at a very high cost for those who were homosexual and denied the opportunity of forming a relationship that would be respected by the wider community. It has come at a cost to men as they have had the sole responsibility of being breadwinners for the family and have not been in a position to negotiate an extended role in parenting. It has been costly for everyone as the churches disapproved of all forms of sexual expression beyond that which occurred within marriage and was required for procreation.

Inglehart, along with other sociologists, has argued that, after World War II, there was a major change in values in the Western world, particularly where the medical advances and the welfare systems were well developed. Another factor at this time was that the contraceptive pill became available. It was approved for distribution in Australia in 1961 and it gave women much greater control over pregnancy. For the first time in human history, for young women of child-bearing age, it gave higher confidence that sex for pleasure could be distinguished from sex for procreation.

A new set of values began to emerge in the 1960s and 1970s in Australia and other Western countries. The duty to family and nation was replaced, to a large extent, by a focus on personal fulfilment. Personal fulfilment could well include family life but could also be found in many other ways: through one's interests, sports, education and careers, for example. It meant that people began exploring how different expressions of intimate relationships could lead to personal fulfilment.

There was an increasing sense that if a marriage did not work out, one should not be bound to it, but should be able to divorce and look for new relationships. This was given government approval in Australia by the *Family Law Act* in 1975 which included a 'no fault' clause allowing people to divorce without having to accuse each other of unfaithfulness. The *Family Law Act* was opposed by the churches, which continued to discourage divorce.

Some felt that the institution of marriage itself was no longer necessary or desirable. They preferred to form relationships as long as it was mutually beneficial, moving out of them as they desired. Others, on the other hand, felt that commitment to the partner in the marriage was desirable for the sake of the security of the children in the family. Over the decades, there has been something of a swing back to valuing marriage as providing some sense of security in the relationship. But it has remained evident to many that, at some level, remaining in a failed or dysfunctional marriage was detrimental to the partners.

The exploration of personal fulfilment in relationships has continued. A major development came in 2016 when the Australian government passed laws allowing same-sex marriages. People could now form life-long committed relationships with people of the same gender. People in same sex relationships could have children and were allowed to adopt children. They could enjoy government benefits such as the absence of death duties. that had previously only been available to married couples of opposite sex.

Again, all Christian denominations were opposed to the proposed law to allow same-sex marriage, apart from the Uniting Church which allowed each presbytery or sector of the church to determine its own stance. The churches argued that they opposed same-sex marriage not only for their own members but for the whole society. While most Australians did not want to enter into such a relationship themselves, they felt that where there was consensual love between two people, they should be allowed to enter a committed and legal relationship. The churches were criticised for their stance not just because of their own values but because of their attempt to impose their own sense of morality on the whole nation. In 2016, two-thirds of all Australians voted in a plebiscite to support same-sex marriages.

According to Inglehart, there was a growing sense in many Western nations that religion was not really about the wellbeing of the individual, but about maintaining the forms of relationship and duties in those relationships which belonged to a bygone age. In an age which valued personal fulfilment, the churches sought to maintain a narrow set of rules, particularly around sexuality and gender roles. Adding to the impact of differentiation and the fading of the influence of religion in many areas of life, the rejection of morality built around family duties has been a major factor in the decline of religion in the Western world since the 1970s. Here, it was not just a case that religious beliefs faded, but that people explicitly rejected the moral teaching of the churches.

Values in production and people

There is another aspect of this change in values which has had an impact on church involvement but which has not been well studied. Since the 1970s, there has been a change in business values. Businesses, particularly state-owned enterprises, which once saw themselves as serving people and serving the nation, have focused on making profits, on serving the shareholders or the owners.

This has been particularly evident in the banking sector. Banks were highly respected social institutions which served their communities. People built relationships with their bank managers and knew that if they needed help financially they could turn to someone they knew to assist them. Indeed, many business people used to attend churches partly because they felt that the churches encouraged honesty in business and fair trading. They felt that the churches provided a moral basis for the business life of the society.

In the 1980s and 1990s, banks such as the Commonwealth Bank in Australia were privatised, and a view emerged that personal relationships between clients and bank managers were not in the banks' best commercial interests. Banks began to move their branch managers around to stop them from forming long-term personal relationships with the members of their community. Decisions could now be made on a less personal basis and more in line with their business objectives.

As the values swung increasingly towards making profits, the churches became more critical of business practices and of the consumerism that businesses were encouraging. Many business people felt caught between what was required of them by their employers and what was encouraged by the churches. Many business people resolved the dilemma by quietly slipping out of the churches. They removed themselves from an environment in which they could not resolve the competing values.

The Anglican Cathedral in Melbourne is now dwarfed by the buildings of the insurance companies, banks and large corporations, illustrating the changed values of contemporary society.

While people's values vary in a multitude of ways, the famous American sociologist Peter Berger in *A Far Glory: The Quest for Faith in an Age of Credulity*, pointed to a basic division in value orientation between what he called the business and the knowledge classes. The business class sees personal fulfilment or success largely in materials terms, in financial gain or in the production of material goods. The knowledge class see personal fulfilment in terms of advances in personal wellbeing, in greater knowledge, better health and stronger community. This latter group tends to have more appreciation of the beauty found in art and nature. Other sociologists working in Europe have affirmed this class distinction and have argued that it is the knowledge class which has taken environmentalism seriously.

The difference between the two groups is visible in different types of occupations. Businesses that have to do with finance, manufacturing, building, distribution and retailing generally measure their success in terms of financial gain and what has been produced.

On the other hand, the health, education and community services sectors see their success in terms of changes in the lives of people, changes that are often small and hard to measure.

The values associated with education, health and community services are more strongly affirmed by the churches than the values associated with business, finance and construction. Indeed, the churches have been active themselves in providing services in the health, education and community service spheres. Research I reported in *Life, Ethics and Faith in Australian Society*, based on the combined data from Australian Surveys of Social Attitudes between 2005 and 2009, found that people associated with those occupations had higher rates of church involvement: 27 per cent of people working in education, and 24 per cent of those working in health attended a church monthly or more often. In contrast, just 16 per cent of plant and machinery operators, 15 per cent of managers, and 14 per cent of people in construction and trades attended a church at that frequency. A high proportion of the people working in the health, education and community service occupations were women.

Raising children also means focusing on the development of children and their wellbeing. Hence, this 'people-orientation' value system explained why more women attended churches than men: it was not a matter of gender *per se*, but of the value system. Confirming this hypothesis, it was found that those men who were working in these people-oriented professions were also more likely to attend a church. Thus 26 per cent of men working in the health sector compared with 23 per cent of women working in the health sector attended a church monthly or more often. The predominance of women in the churches was due to more women having this value orientation.

More recent research has suggested, however, that the lines are not quite as clear as they may have been. There has been increasing pressure in education and health, for example, to move into a mindset in which success is measured by numerical indicators of performance – such as cost per patient in the health system or the Naplan results in the education system. Moreover, there are also many men working in business and construction who deeply value relationships and family life and feel that the growth of people is important.

Duty and personal fulfilment

People who were born in the Western world in the 1920s and 1930s went through the Great Depression and then World War II. They survived because they learnt to be thrifty, to abstain from luxuries, and to give themselves dutifully to the nation in war. They survived because families stuck together through the difficult times and supported each other.

However, it was different for those who grew up in the 1950s and 1960s. This was a boom time in Australia. The possibilities of life were opening up. People could spend money for a better life. Free university places in the 1970s made it possible for many to climb the social ladders through advanced education. World travel was made much easier as flights became cheap enough for the average person. International and civil conflicts were sufficiently rare to allow travel to become available to most parts of the world. It was the time when people could dream and see their dreams realised. As women entered the workforce alongside men, they gained economic independence and the ability to realise dreams for their own lives.

This focus on personal fulfilment did not necessarily mean that people became selfish. Certainly, it was easy for this ambition to slide into selfish individualism, as is recognised when people talk about the 'me generation'. Yet, in every survey, when people were asked about what was most important in life for them, family and friends head the list. More than anything, people want relationships in which there is care and respect, in which there is security but also fun. Most people find their deepest fulfilment in their closest relationships. They recognise that within those relationships there must be some give and take. We can help each other to enjoy life. When someone is in a close relationship just for their own pleasure, that relationship quickly disintegrates.

There are many broken families in the Western world today. Fulfilling relationships have not always been sustained. One might wonder whether relationships were more secure and perhaps better when duty dominated. Yet, the plea of Tevye to his wife in *Fiddler on the Roof* resounds through the century: Do you love me? It is not enough that Golde has made his bed, cooked his meals, and washed his clothes. Relationships can be deeper and more fulfilling. While there are many relationships which have not worked out, there are also many which are deeper and more fulfilling than they have ever been.

I see the same pattern in relationships between parents and children. While sometimes relationships break and children go their own way, there are many cases where adult children and their parents continue to enjoy a strong relationship of love and care. It is not unusual for parents and their adult children to say of each other that they are 'best friends'. They continue to find fulfilment in each other when the duties of care of parent for a child are no longer relevant.

The idea of personal fulfilment is also apparent in attitudes towards work. Most people want more from the workplace than money. They want work that is interesting and enjoyable. They want respectful, even enjoyable, relationships in the workplace. They look for work which will use their capacities and enhance their skills and which will contribute towards a fulfilling career.

People approach other involvements with similar attitudes. They are happy to give something of themselves in the things they do, but they also expect to get something out of it, whether it be involvement in sport, in a club that revolves around a hobby, or in a church. Duty will not keep them involved very long if they do not find it fun and fulfilling for themselves.

The duty to attend religious services is not enough to engage people. Certainly, some may find enjoyment in the music, the liturgy and the preaching. But that is not enough. People look for opportunities to form fulfilling relationships within their religious communities. They may also look for ways they can extend their skills and contribute to others through playing musical instruments or in taking over meaningful roles. When such opportunities are not present, or when relationships are not formed, then people are not likely to continue to attend.

The Boomer generation, born between 1946 and 1964 was the first Australian generation to cease attending religious services in large numbers. It was not just the case that they ceased to hold on to religious beliefs or engage in religious practices. They often found that their emphasis on personal fulfilment and their ways of finding it were not affirmed within churches. Over subsequent years, those trends away from religion have strengthened.

Many people in the Western world have greatly appreciated the freedom they have found over the last 50 years. They have felt that they have broken free from the restrictions which religion has attempted to impose on them. However, there are some who have continued to find a sense of safety and security in religion. They have looked to religion to provide greater security in their marriages. They have argued that the sense of duty to family has provided a secure foundation for family life and their children's development. While many people have chosen to commit themselves to their families so their children can enjoy the good things in life, some have continued to value religious faith for its reinforcement of those family-oriented values.

The values that have centred on human wellbeing have been articulated by various philosophers. 'Humanistic' was used for Christian theologians who focused on human wellbeing. However, secular humanism, which stressed the use of science and scientific methods in determining the best ways of enhancing human wellbeing, has been developed by philosophers such as John Dewey and Julian Huxley in the 20th century. Humanism has emphasised the importance of human beings taking responsibility for their own future, and has been critical of religion as encouraging reliance on God or on supernatural forces. Humanist philosophers have played a role in providing a coherent alternative to religious values.

Spirituality

Over recent years, surveys have found that close to one quarter of the Australian population, and many people in populations across the Western world, have described themselves as 'spiritual but not religious'. Some religious groups have warmly welcomed this news. They have seen it as evidence that we are not descending entirely into a secular abyss.

In 2005, two British researchers at Lancaster University, Paul Heelas and Linda Woodhead, published an important book *The Spiritual Revolution: Why Religion Is Giving Way to Spirituality*. It was an in-depth study of people in a town in England which detailed how spirituality was expressed. Many of these people were involved in yoga, tai chi and meditation. Heelas and Woodhead saw this as a development of the New Age phenomenon which emerged in the 1960s and as a 'successor' to traditional religion.

It is certainly true that many people think it is important to 'nurture the self' and they do this in a great many ways, which will be explored more in chapters seven and eight. Two-thirds of the Australians who refer to themselves as being 'spiritual but not religious' are people who used to attend a church but do so no longer. They are probably indicating that, while they are no longer religious, this does not mean that such nurturing is no longer important to them. These people are varied. Some of them continue to believe in God or in a higher being. Others do not share those beliefs but are agnostic or atheistic. Whether people use the language of spirituality or not, the idea of nurturing the self in one way or another, in doing things that contribute to one's enjoyment of life and one's sense of wellbeing, is common throughout the population. Secularisation certainly does not mean a rigid materialism that gives no thought to one's wellbeing.

On the other hand, spirituality outside of religion has not become a distinct movement taking the place of religion. People will find many ways of enhancing their lives and use language in a variety of ways to describe it. Some people may find the language of spirituality helpful. Others may talk simply about wellbeing. Secularisation refers specifically to the decline of religion, religious institutions and their dogmas, and the use of the language of spirituality does not mean secularisation is not occurring.

Has the decline in church involvement produced a moral vacuum?

Christianity has not only promoted the value of duty to family and community. It has also taught people to be compassionate towards each other. It has been the inspiration for many to give time, money and effort to help those who are less fortunate. It has led to the formation of many charities and contributed to community programs to promote a caring society.

In *The Economic Impact of Religion on Society in Australia: Recent Research and Commentary*, edited by A. Keith Thompson, and published in 2023, clear evidence is provided that those who attend a church volunteer more. It has been argued by some researchers that this additional volunteering was just in the churches and just for those who were members of those churches. However, recent research has shown that this is not true. Church attenders also volunteer more in the wider community. While Australian adults who do not attend church spend, on average, 6.1 hours per month in volunteering in the wider community, those who attend a church monthly or more often spend 10.7 hours a month volunteering in the wider community.

Across Australia, this difference in the hours of volunteering has been estimated to be worth $1,350 million to the Australian economy per year. Religious attenders volunteer significantly more than non-attenders in the areas of welfare and community services, in youth, children and parenting organisations and in education and training. In other areas of volunteering, such as emergency services, sports and physical recreation, arts, music and drama, for example, religious attenders' rates of volunteering are similar to those of non-attenders.

However, further evidence showed that being raised to volunteer, practising volunteering as a child and having it modelled by parents in the home had a greater impact than religion on the practice of volunteering as an adult. Analysis also suggested that it was not primarily the religious beliefs that had a major effect but that religious groups provided an opportunity for people to invite each other to volunteer. They created opportunities for the engagement of volunteers. Indeed, religious groups frequently began their own welfare activities for the wider community and engaged their own members in assisting.

The *Contributing to Australian Society* survey, on which this analysis of volunteering was based, conducted in 2016, asked people about informal care for others outside their families. In almost all areas, the religious were significantly more likely that the non-religious to report that they had helped people in, for example, providing transport or running errands, in teaching and coaching, in providing emotional support and using specialised or professional skills to help others. However, further analysis suggested that while religion was a significant factor in people helping others, age and educational background were also factors. It was suggested by the researchers that the major factor in offering care is being directly confronted with the needs of others. Most Australians will help others if they are aware of the need and are in a position to offer assistance.

The survey showed that most people, whether they attend a church or not, want to contribute to the wellbeing of others and find personal satisfaction in doing so. Knowing others will benefit, if they have the skills and opportunity, they will do what they can to help. Some people, such as Richard Dawkins, have argued that evolution made us all competitors in the struggle for the 'survival of the fittest'. But others have argued, including Darwin himself, that many animals, including Homo sapiens, have an innate 'social instinct' which leads them to feel sympathy for and seek the companionship of other members of their species.

Evolution has taught human beings to have empathy for each other. Stefan Klein, a researcher and scientific journalist, has argued in his book, *Survival of the Nicest: How Altruism Made Us Human and Why It Pays to Get Along*, that "characteristics such as amiability, gentleness, and helpfulness developed because they gave their possessors an advantage in evolutionary competition" (p. 92). In the long run, there is an advantage to helping others. Groups tend to exclude those who are freeloaders and try to get away with not contributing to the wellbeing of the group. There is a widespread recognition that all human beings should be treated fairly and with compassion, although it is taking a long time to recognise the basic equality of all human beings.

Religion has contributed significantly to encouraging compassion and altruism, and, perhaps more importantly, has actively engaged people in charitable activities to benefit others. The decline in religion is having some impact on the extent of volunteering in Australia. However, the decline in religion does not mean that we descend into selfish competition. Nor does it mean that there is no motivation for people to be kind and generous to others. In all human societies, people have helped each other, although there have generally been significant differences between those people they were willing to help and those, perhaps outside their group, they were not willing to help. There has long been racism, sexism, ageism, and distinctions of social class despite, and sometimes because of, religious teaching.

The decline of religion does not necessarily mean the decline of compassion and altruism. The individual pursuit of personal fulfilment does not equal selfishness. People know that, in most instances, they will find fulfilment as they are able to share their goals and their journeys with others. They know that they are most likely to achieve what they want if they collaborate with others and help others out. They know that, in the long run, they will be helped by others if they offer assistance to others when they see a need that they are in a position to meet.

In summary

Advances in medical science have led to a decline in infant mortality. Advances in national welfare systems have given people a greater sense of security, including for their old age. In those countries which have benefitted from these changes, the importance of duty to family life has weakened and has been replaced by an emphasis on personal fulfilment. This quest for personal fulfilment was evident in the feminist movement which emerged in the 1960s and 1970s. It has been evident in the different ways in which people have sought to construct their relationships with each other, culminating in Australia in 2016 in the decision to allow same-sex marriages. It has been evident in the ways people look for a fulfilling career through their work. Most churches have opposed these developments in values and have continued to argue for those values which protect family structures and which emphasise gender specific roles. When people have rejected those values, so they have rejected the churches which have promoted them.

It is recognised that the churches have also promoted the values of altruism as shown in volunteerism and many people continue to find the churches provide ways in which they can contribute to the wellbeing of others and the wider society. Nevertheless, most Australians do respond positively to needs when they are confronted with a specific need which they have the ability to meet.

Western societies in which most people are seeking their own ways of personal fulfilment are developing a different set of values to support people's agendas. It is to those social agendas that we now turn.

Chapter 4

Changes in Society's Values

Social values and social cohesion

Apart from the values of individuals which direct their activities and determine their behaviour, societies are governed by values, often reinforced through laws, for their smooth operation. Societies require conformity to these values for the benefit of the whole society. The nature of that conformity varies, however, from one society to another. As individual values change, so changes are required in societal values. In times of war or economic depression, the liberty of the members of the society is curtailed. The society requires that everyone share in the challenges. When there is economic prosperity, individuals can be given more freedom. The focus on personal fulfilment since the 1970s in Australia and many Western countries has led to new values for how society should operate. This chapter will explore these new values and how they have come into conflict with religious values.

Human societies have commonly thought that all their members should have the same religion. People of other religions were seen as a threat. They could not be trusted as they saw the world in a different way. They had different values. Thus, many societies have taken steps to remove people of different religions, to expel them, to kill them, or at the very least, limit their power. The Spanish Inquisitions in the 13th and 14th centuries are a particular example as many thousands of Muslims, Jews and Christians who were regarded as holding heretical beliefs were persecuted, tortured, and in some cases killed, as recently described by Helen Rawlings in her detailed book of this era. This suspicion of other religions continues in different ways and in different contexts. Amongst the more extreme contemporary expressions are the repressions of the Tibetans and the Uyghurs by the Han Chinese and of the Rohingya by the Burmese.

Yet, there are many examples where people of different faiths have lived together peacefully and productively. Not long before the Spanish Inquisitions began, Christians, Jews and Muslims were living together peacefully under the regimes of the Islamic Nasrid dynasty in Granada and other parts of Spain. For centuries, Muslims, Hindus, Buddhists, Sikhs and people of other faiths have lived together in India.

All contemporary Western societies are constituted of people of different faiths and ideologies, the consequence of widespread immigration. The diversity has been extended by the great variety of ways in which people have sought personal fulfilment. People in same-sex marriages can live alongside people in other-sex marriages, just as people who find fulfilment in sport live alongside people who find that fulfilment in art. People who enjoy classical music live alongside people who enjoy popular music.

Societies do need some common conventions by which all of their members must abide. It would be chaos if every individual could decide which side of the road to drive a car, or if everyone could simply put up their own dwelling wherever they wanted. But there are other areas of life where we can follow our personal preferences without undermining society as a whole.

One of the essential values in a society in which personal fulfilment is the preeminent personal value is tolerance. Members of such societies need to be tolerant of those who have chosen a different path of life to themselves, of those who have different goals and who seek personal fulfilment in different ways from their own. While it is important that people seek to persuade others of particular values or behaviours where the common good is at stake, in many areas of life which do not involve harm to others, there is a widespread attitude that it is wrong to force others to conform to one's own ideals. Intolerance becomes intolerable in society when people are trying to coerce others. Just recently, in Australia, a mother was jailed for forcing her daughter to enter a marriage she did not want, and in which she was killed by her partner. Arranged marriages are permitted, if the person to be married consents to the arrangement, but forcing people against their will is not allowed by law.

Tolerance of diversity

Indeed, it is not just tolerance that is valued, but the affirmation of diversity. In contemporary societies, diversity in the ways in which people live, engage in different sports, have different interests, and pursue different ways of life is encouraged. Our society prizes the diversity from having different designs for our homes through to personalising the screens on our phones. People love the diversity in the cuisines that are now available in most parts of the Western world.

A major value that has emerged in contemporary Western societies is consent. This is particularly important in sexual relationships where the idea of consent has not always been at the forefront in people's minds and control has been common. In a society in which all people are equally entitled to find their own personal fulfilment, consent between partners is essential. The emphasis on consent has shone a light on the evil of domestic abuse. It is now seen as wrong for one person to seek to control a partner financially or psychologically as well as physically. The value of consent in relationships and the evil of trying to control or coerce one's partner has come to be commonly accepted. Consent was not the focus in the values of family life in the age of duty when it was common for women to be told to put up with the behaviour of an abusive partner for the sake of the marriage.

Similar values are important in employer-employee relationships. Employers cannot coerce their employees to do specific things, especially engage in behaviour which is dangerous, without consent. Employers can be and are held to account for harm which befalls an employee. Over time, trade unions have driven changes in what employers can expect of their employees. Negotiations occur within complex sets of regulations. Within this process of negotiation, there is often an imbalance of power. Unions have provided mechanisms for collective bargaining. Laws have been made to protect the processes of negotiation for the best outcome for both the employer and the employee.

Constraints to avoid harming others

There are important social limits to tolerance in the individual pursuit of personal fulfilment. If that pursuit has a harmful impact on the ability of others to pursue their own personal fulfilment, then it must be limited. Many aspects of life are carefully regulated to ensure that we do not harm the rights of others. If we build a house that is much higher than those around us, which cuts the light reaching our neighbours or which hides the views they had, it may not be acceptable. So, in building a house, it is important that the plans are made public, the impact on others is assessed and neighbours have the opportunity to object.

A child goes to kindergarten with his lunch box. He shares his lunch with his friends. But the lunch contains sandwiches of peanut butter. His friend has a life-threatening anaphylaxis reaction. Thus, even the lunch that a child brings to kindergarten must be regulated.

In general, the individual pursuit of personal fulfilment must be curtailed when it could harm others. Our society certainly does not give *carte blanche* to whatever people want to do. The consequences of people's actions must be considered. Even when people directly harm only themselves, that harm often has costs to the wider society and society bears the consequences. Smoking can lead to a range of physical ailments and can shorten one's life. At one level, it is a personal decision, but it has implications for society. Thus, governments have been encouraging people not to smoke and raising the cost of doing so through the tax system. Ultimately, by discouraging smoking, the cost to the whole society for health care will be reduced.

Societies vary greatly in the extent to which they regulate the behaviour of their members. It is often difficult to draw the line between allowing people to follow whatever path they want to take to personal fulfilment and what needs to be regulated for the common good. That line must be negotiated by those present in the society, looking at the costs of allowing diversity compared to the consequences of limiting freedom.

Equality of opportunity

One of the great principles of contemporary society is that there should be equality of opportunity for people to follow their own paths to personal fulfilment. This means that there should be no restrictions on the basis of gender. This has been a major change for the most recent generations. There have been sectors of society which have closed their doors to women. Women have not been allowed to take on certain occupations, and some religious organisations are amongst the continuing offenders here. Women have not had opportunity to participate in certain sports or enter certain clubs. Gradually, those restrictions are disappearing, although it is a slower process to achieve equality of pay for equal work.

Equality of opportunity means that there should be no discrimination against people of a different race. Cases are often reported where police, for example, appear to have treated people of different racial backgrounds differently. It is sometimes asserted that the high rates in incarceration of Aboriginal Australians reflects discrimination in policing. People may be treated differently in schools or in the health system, in the housing market or on public transport.

The basic principle of equality of opportunity is being applied to people with disability. They are entitled to be employed in jobs they are able to do. Public facilities – whether it be transport or the local public library – need to be constructed so they can be accessed and used by people with a disability. Our society takes these things seriously, although how to provide people with disability equal opportunities in the workforce or in sport or housing, for example, is complex and only gradually being worked out. Age can also be a basis for discrimination, for instance, in the workplace.

Homophobia

People in homosexual relationships still struggle for equality of opportunity. While the Commonwealth government has adopted the principle that homosexual couples should have equal legal rights to marriage and to other benefits, it is only right that they should have equal rights in employment and in other sectors of society.

Yet, this is something that some church organisations have opposed. Christian schools have sought to have the right to sack a teacher who is in a homosexual relationship. Indeed, some schools have even asked their parents to affirm their intolerance of homosexuality. They argue that they should have the right to refuse employment to someone who does not act in accordance with the moral principles they advocate. On the other hand, when the homosexual teacher is teaching something which is quite neutral to his or her personal preference for a homosexual lifestyle, and that choice has no impact on his or her ability to do the job that is required, why should they not have the opportunity to teach?

It is not an easy issue to resolve: the rights of employers to hold their employees to their values over against the rights of employees to choose their own (legal) ways of pursuing their personal fulfilment. The issue could be seen by the church organisation as one of potential harm as it considers homosexuality 'harmful'. But Australian society, in general, does not agree. While an individual may decide for themselves whether to adopt a homosexual lifestyle, society affirms the right of people to make their own decision, and that employing organisations should no longer have the right to sack people who engage personally in a homosexual lifestyle.

What does this have to do with secularisation?

Over the course of the past 50 years, many Western nations have developed laws and regulations based on moral codes which are quite different from the traditional moral codes promulgated by religious bodies. The conflict between these moral codes is reinforcing the processes of secularisation in society. The conflict has demonstrated the limitations of the systems of morality which have their roots in religion. Indeed, after centuries of being the moral leaders, there have been instances where nations and states have taken that role and have condemned the religious groups for their moral failings. This has been apparent in national responses to sexual abuse in religious organisations, for example. The adoption in society of moral codes different from those affirmed by religious groups has contributed to a significant loss of confidence in the religious groups and religious institutions.

There is potential for conflict at the very heart of the change in values. Religions in general and the churches in particular have emphasised the importance of duty to family and community and lauded the sacrifice of the self for others. The values which evolved in the West in the 1950s and 1960s emphasised personal fulfilment, which, for many people, meant personal enjoyment and pleasure. Nowhere was the conflict so strong as in relation to sexuality. With modern birth control, sex could be enjoyed for the pleasure that it gave, and not just as a duty within family that would lead to the birth of children.

The social values of tolerance and affirmation of diversity which have developed in societies where personal fulfilment is paramount conflict with the traditional religious values of duty to family and nation.

Over the centuries, the sense of duty – expressed in the suppression of personal ambition and obedience to one's superiors – has been evident in many religious communities. It was demonstrated, for example, in some religious orders of monks and nuns who were expected to lead highly ordered lives in which their personal ambitions were suppressed. In the past, and in some places in a continuing way, it has been expressed through the requirement for all members of a religious order to wear identical forms of dress which hid personal characteristics.

There was no sense of equality in these communities, nor in many religious communities around the world, both Christian and those of other religions. In some churches today that sense of hierarchy remains in which people are expected to be obedient to those who are senior to them and where there is little opportunity to question the decisions of the leadership. In a recent study of young people leaving Pentecostal churches by Mark Bohr the authoritarian attitudes of some leaders in the churches and the lack of opportunity for debate was one of the reasons people gave for leaving the churches.

Another area of conflict between the values of the wider Australian society and the values of the churches has been in relation to the equality of women and men. It is taught in some church communities that males should be leaders and make the decisions, both in the religious communities and in the homes. Women are taught that they should submit to the leadership of men. There is certainly a danger here that men who have a tendency to abuse others are attracted into communities which support those ideas. The inequality in terms of gender in many religious communities is one of the factors which has led to a low level of confidence in the churches. While some churches maintain that they are only talking about roles rather than a hierarchy, that ultimately males and females are equal before God, it is hard for the wider community not to see it as inequality when females are forbidden to take equal roles in leadership and decision-making.

The fact that many religious communities also condemn homosexuality and exclude people in homosexual relationships is another area where the morality of the majority of Australians conflicts with the morality practised in many religious communities. Few churches in Australia, even now, permit same-sex marriages in their churches. Catholics, Anglicans, Baptists, Churches of Christ and other denominations have forbidden their clergy to celebrate or, in some cases, to bless same-sex marriages. Many churches prohibit people in same-sex relationships from taking leadership roles in their churches. Again, from the point of view of many in the wider society, this is seen as conflicting with the basic rules of respecting the personal ways of life of all people, if they do not harm others.

However, another issue has arisen which was not so much a conflict of values but society accusing the churches of not adhering to basic human values. As reports of the abuse of children within religious communities arose in the late 20th century and early 21st century in many countries around the world, people were horrified. The huge harm that it has caused is well documented. When it happened in schools, sporting clubs and other sectors of society, it was regarded as horrific. When it happened within religious communities which claimed to be taking the moral lead in society and which had been trusted with the care of the young, it was especially grievous.

While it is to be expected that secularisation would gather momentum as the importance of God in people's lives faded, the child abuse that was uncovered within religious communities added significantly to its momentum. What made the wider community even more angry was the attempts to cover up the cases of child abuse, to move priests who were known to be offending from one place to another, giving them further opportunity for abuse. It became apparent that this cover up extended right through the hierarchy of denominations, and Anglican and Catholic bishops, for example, have been put on trial for their part in the cover up.

In Australia, the state took action through the formation of the Royal Commission on the Institutional Responses to Child Sexual Abuse in 2016. Thousands of cases in churches and church-run institutions were identified. The stories were told and the ways in which churches had tried to cover up these abuses were identified. The Royal Commission made it very clear that this evil had to be stopped and set up a number of procedures which the churches and other organisations had to follow in order to prevent it from occurring again. People working with children were required to have police checks and state-based specific 'working with children' checks. Mandatory reporting of child abuse to the police was introduced. Churches were expected to change their culture to prevent such abuse from re-occurring.

Systems have been established to give people who have been abused some recompense for their suffering and churches were required to come to participate in these arrangements. However, many cases have come to the courts and will continue to come to the courts. Some church authorities have fought these cases for compensation, even when the cases have been proven in the courts. In one notorious case in Sydney in 2018, the Catholic Archdiocese of Sydney pleaded that it was not an incorporated entity, so it could not be sued, now referred to as the Ellis Defence. The Archdiocese won that case. But it led to some Australian states taking further action requiring churches to set up incorporated entities so that they could be sued. The legislation gives the power to the courts to sue the trust that legally holds the titles of property if this is necessary.

It was a dramatic reversal. The churches, which had been seen as moral leaders in society, had been revealed as wrongdoers not only in the abuse but in failing to report abuse and attempting to cover it up. The state took the moral high ground, in listening to those who had been abused, punishing abusers, and seeking some redress for survivors.

The *Australian Survey of Social Attitudes* in 2018 found that confidence in the churches and religious organisations had fallen considerably. Just 11 per cent of the population continued to have a great amount or complete confidence in the churches, down from 22 per cent in 2009. In just nine years, confidence levels had halved. The decline in confidence has been occurring for several decades now. In 1983, more than half of the population had at least some confidence in the churches and religious organisations.

Further analysis identified some of the factors in these low levels of confidence. The first and most significant was that most Australians regard the churches as having too much power, affirmed by 62 per cent of those surveyed. The churches were seen to have too much power in the ways they have sought to cover up the cases of abuse. However, the power issue has also come to the fore through recent discussion about laws to protect religion from discrimination. The ways that the churches tried to wield influence in the plebiscite on same-sex marriage was also seen as an abuse of their power. The power of the churches and religious organisations is also seen in their property, their financial resources, their political and even legal power, and in the fact that their schools, hospitals and many other institutions gain much of their funding from the government.

Closely associated with this concern about their power is the belief that religion has contributed more to war than to peace. In the 2018 *Australian Survey of Social Attitudes*, this was affirmed by 72 per cent of Australian adults. It is probable that most people had in mind some of the conflicts overseas, particularly the conflict in Northern Ireland which was usually framed in terms of Catholics versus Protestants. They probably had in mind also the terrorist attacks on the Twin Towers in New York and the subsequent terrorist attacks in the name of religion in other parts of the world.

Another issue which had a significant, although lesser, impact on the lack of confidence in churches and religious organisations was that these institutions were seen as barriers to the equality of women in society. It was affirmed by 50 per cent of the national sample of Australian adults.

Interestingly, the survey showed that 70 per cent of Australian adults affirmed the statement that people with strong religious views were intolerant of others. However, in itself, when the concerns about the churches' power, the perception that religion contributed more to violence than to peace, and the lack of equality for women were taken into account, the perception of intolerance added little to the overall lack of confidence.

Analysis also showed that those people who did not believe in God had less confidence in churches and religious organisations, as did those who had little confidence for society's institutions generally. However, the lack of confidence was not just a matter of people rejecting religious teaching. It was more a matter of feeling that the churches and religious organisations more generally have failed in relation to contemporary moral standards. The hierarchical view of society, the emphasis on conformity and obedience in the churches and other religious organisations conflicts directly with the values of equality, especially between females and males, of tolerance and affirmation of diversity, and of the importance of mutual consent in relationships.

The environment

There are other conflicts between the moral values which have emerged in contemporary society and those of the churches. A major moral challenge which has come to the fore in the latter part of the 20th century is that of global warming. Science has pointed to the fact that the planet is warming at a rapid rate, largely due to the impact of human activity such as the burning of fossil fuels. This warming is creating not just more frequent and more intense heat-waves and droughts, but in some places more violent storms and floods and more frequent tornadoes. Global warming is having a huge impact on human life around the globe as well as on many species of plants and animals. It is threatening the survival of the Great Barrier Reef off Australia's eastern coast and many species of plants and animals which have been dependent on the snows in Australia's high country.

In a famous 1967 paper by an American historian, Lynn White, the claim was made that Christian beliefs lay at the root of ecological problems because Christians had developed the idea that the earth had been created by God for human beings to use for their own purposes. Research that I did in Australia in 1997 found that many Christians did feel that the earth was simply there for human use. However, many other Christians responded that the true teaching was that human beings have been given the responsibility for the care of creation.

Indeed, many Christian and other religious groups have been active in the environmental movement. Many institutions have made statements and formed bodies to promote the environment such as Catholic Earthcare. Nevertheless, the survey data has consistently shown that Christians in Australia are divided about the importance of the care of the environment. In 2022, Stephen Reid, co-ordinator of research at the Christian Research Association, Australia, reported data from the 2020 *Australian Survey of Social Attitudes* that 63 per cent of church attenders were concerned or very concerned about the environment, compared with 73 per cent of people who never attended a church. Eleven per cent of church attenders indicated they had little or no concern about environmental issues. Overall, Christians have not taken a leadership role in this huge moral challenge. It is another aspect of modern life in which the moral priorities of the churches have been in contrast to the moral priorities of the wider society.

Serving the community

While the reasons have been presented in this chapter why many have left the churches and other religious organisations, there is another side to the story which should be noted again. All major religious organisations promote compassion and the principle that we should treat others as we wish to be treated ourselves. While recognising that religious organisations have failed at various times to live up to their own moral standards, apart from having different standards on some issues to the societies in which they are situated, they have all encouraged pro-social behaviour. In particular, religious organisations have been at the forefront of caring for the vulnerable for millennia and continue to do so in Australia today.

There are a multitude of small and large programs which have been initiated by churches, for example, to provide shelter for the homeless and food for the hungry, to care for asylum seekers and other immigrants, to assist people with a disability and the frail aged and those who care for them. NCLS Research has noted that in 2021, 48 per cent of local churches offered some emergency or material relief and 23 per cent provided some forms of counselling services. As reported in *The Economic Impact of Religion on Society in Australia*, those who attend churches not only give more to their communities through volunteering but also through donations to charitable causes. Indeed, some people continue to be engaged in the churches because they find opportunities through them to expression their compassion and to contribute to the wellbeing of the wider society.

Associated with all the major denominations are large, professionally-run welfare organisations such as Catholicare, Anglicare, Baptcare, and Uniting. They provide a multitude of welfare services which are used widely by the general public. The *Contribution to Australian Society* survey found that 60 per cent of adult Australians had some or much confidence in these charitable organisations, compared with 61 per cent with some or much confidence in charities not associated with churches.

In 2024 in Australia, 85 hospitals were operated by Christian churches providing around 12,000 hospital beds. Christian churches also run numerous aged care facilities around the country.

A large portion of education is provided by Christian organisations. According to the Australian Bureau of Statistics, in 2023, 19.7 per cent of all students attended a Catholic school, and another 16.3 per cent attended an independent school, most of which had some Christian affiliation. One of the reasons for the continuing popularity of Christian schools is the pastoral care that they offer and their attention to the needs of the individual.

In summary

There have been significant changes in the social values in Western societies since the 1970s as personal values have shifted from a focus on duty to family and community towards a more individualised focus on personal fulfilment. A society which supports personal fulfilment is a society which is tolerant and allows people freedom to find what is fulfilling to them, in contrast to the common religious expectation of conformity and obedience. Such a society highly values equality so that each person, within their context, can seek that fulfilment. This contrasts with the sense of hierarchy and obedience to those who are higher in the social ladder common in some churches.

The secularisation of Western societies has not meant that moral values have declined. Rather, the moral values have changed. Some behaviours which were seen as moral evils, such as homosexuality, have now been generally accepted as not evil at all. Other behaviours which were often hidden, or received little attention, such as domestic abuse and child abuse, have now been identified as great evils.

There are some stark contrasts between the moral values traditionally upheld by the churches compared with those promoted by contemporary society. Conformity has been replaced by tolerance of diversity. Obedience has been replaced by responsibility and consent. Duty to family and community has been replaced by the search for personal fulfilment. At the same time, contemporary Western societies are very aware that the search for personal fulfilment was often found in family and networks of friends and must be expressed in ways which do not harm or restrict others in that search. In particular, consent is vital in all relationships.

There is also a great moral challenge which is seen as hanging over the whole of society: that of responding to global warming and climate change. It is a trend which could spell the end of human existence, certainly as we know it. Again, this is a moral challenge on which some churches have been largely silent or have even promulgated climate denial. On the other hand, other churches have certainly addressed climate change and have interpreted their faith in terms of their responsibility to the protection of the planet. However, it has been mostly people outside the churches who have led the world in seeking to address this on-going challenge.

The sphere of individual and social morality is not one like science in which God has faded and become irrelevant. Rather it is a sphere of conflict between the moral systems of the churches and the emerging moral systems of the Western world. It has left many Western people angry at the churches and religion: angry at the failure to give equality to women, angry at the wars in which religions have been complicit and motivated hatred, and angry at the abuses that have occurred. The perceived failures of the religious moral systems have contributed significantly to the secularisation process.

On the other hand, there remains a respect for the Christian value of compassion. While many people no longer attend churches, they continue to use welfare programs initiated and operated by parishes, and the services of the welfare agencies, hospitals and schools. And many people continue to volunteer and contribute to these services.

Chapter 5

Immigration and Secularisation

The roles of religion in the immigration process

Immigration is having a huge impact on the religious profile of most Western nations. One of the first places immigrants go when they arrive in a new country is their religious community. It is a place where they can be sure to meet others who come from the same background, who speak their language and who share their customs. In the highly multicultural countries of the West, there are thousands of small and large religious communities of every cultural group represented among them.

A Chinese temple and a Cambodian temple back-to-back in the suburbs of Melbourne serving two of Australia's many immigrant communities.

As a result of immigration, the religious profile of most Western countries has become much more diverse than it has ever been. Hindus from various parts of India, Nepal, Fiji and other places, gather in temples and community centres. Islamic mosques, large and small, have sprung up throughout the Western world. Buddhist temples can be found in towns and monasteries in rural areas, offering opportunities not only for communities to meet, but for people to learn and practise meditation. Sikh gurdwaras provide their communities a place for honouring the Guru Granth Sahib and for forming community over langar, the common meal.

These communities play an important role for immigrants. Not only do they provide community for new arrivals, but they provide assistance in settling into the new environment: how to find employment, how to work the banking system, for example. Frequently, they provide classes in the Western language or point to where such classes can be found, just as they provide classes in the languages of the immigrant group to assist immigrant parents with maintaining their culture.

There have been some Christians who have blamed the newly arrived religions for the decline of Christian faith. They have seen these religions grow while Christianity declines. While these other religions have certainly changed the religious profile, their impact has actually been to raise the matter of religion in the mind of the public. They have brought religion into the public arena as the management of the diversity of religions is considered.

A school chaplain in a government-run school in a large city told me about the influx of immigrant students into the school. They had religious rules which meant changes in their uniforms. They wanted times for prayer during the school day. These matters were easily accommodated, but it had raised the consciousness about religion among other students. Did they themselves have a religion? Did it mean anything to them?

The impact of immigration on the religious profile

However, the impact on the Christian communities from immigration was much greater than raising consciousness about religion. In most Western countries, a large proportion of the immigrants have been Christian. Thus, immigration has directly boosted Christian numbers. The Australian Bureau of Statistics provides the religious identity of the immigrants who arrived in Australia between 2017 and 2021. In round figures, there were:

- 290,00 Christians
- 177,000 Hindus
- 101,000 Muslims
- 78,000 Buddhists
- 48,000 Sikhs, and
- 3,000 Jews.

There were also 288,000 immigrants who described themselves as having no religion.

The impact on the Christian profile has occurred in two major ways. First, new Christian denominations have arrived. In the 1960s, in Australia, the Reformed Church was founded bringing with it its history of involvement in Christian education. Since then, a range of Christian churches from the Middle East have become established such as the Coptic Orthodox from Egypt, the Assyrian Orthodox, the Ancient Church of the East and the Syrian Jacobite Church. With these new churches has come a new vitality and a desire to bring up their children in the traditions which they have held for millennia. New congregations have been established and new theological colleges and monasteries have been built.

In other cases, new local congregations have been formed within existing churches. Every week, the Mass is celebrated in more than 30 languages in Catholic Churches in Melbourne. There are numerous congregations with their own language, celebrating their faith and their community. The same applies to most denominations. The Baptists have had a long history of forming immigrant congregations. After World War II, they formed Baptist congregations of Romanians and Serbs, Russians and Dutch, and of people from many other European nations. Later came the Vietnamese Baptists, and, most recently, congregations from Myanmar including the Chin and the Karen have formed. The Presbyterians and The Uniting Church have strong Korean congregations as well as Chinese and Islander congregations. The Anglicans have congregations of Sudanese, Somali, Indonesian, Indian and Iranian people. The Seventh-day Adventists have Islander congregations from Tonga and Samoa.

For some decades, the largest group of Christian immigrants has been Catholic, benefitting from the strength of Catholicism around the world. Between 2017 and 2021, 150,000 Catholics arrived in Australia. They came from the Philippines, India, Hong Kong, and a great variety of other countries in Africa, Asia, Oceania, South, North and Central America, as well as Europe. Over that same period,

- 20,000 Anglicans arrived,
- 16,000 Baptists,
- 11,000 Pentecostals,
- 10,000 Presbyterian and Reformed,
- 8,000 Eastern Orthodox,
- 8,000 Oriental Orthodox and Assyrian Apostolic,
- 6,000 Uniting Church, and
- 4,000 Seventh-day Adventists.

Almost every denomination benefitted, although some much more than others.

Immigration is thus a major factor which is slowing down the process of secularisation in Australia. Figure 2 shows the effect of that for the major Christian denominations between 2011 and 2021. The dark bars show what the decline in each denomination would have been without immigration and the lighter bars show what the decline actually was with immigration. For example, the Catholic population would have declined by 13 per cent without immigrants. The immigrants reduced the decline to just 7 per cent. Overall, the number of people identifying with a Christian denomination declined by 15 per cent between 2011 and 2021, but it would have declined by more than 20 per cent if it was not for immigration.

Figure 2. The Change in Numbers Identifying with Various Christian Denominations between 2011 and 2021 with and without the Impact of Immigration

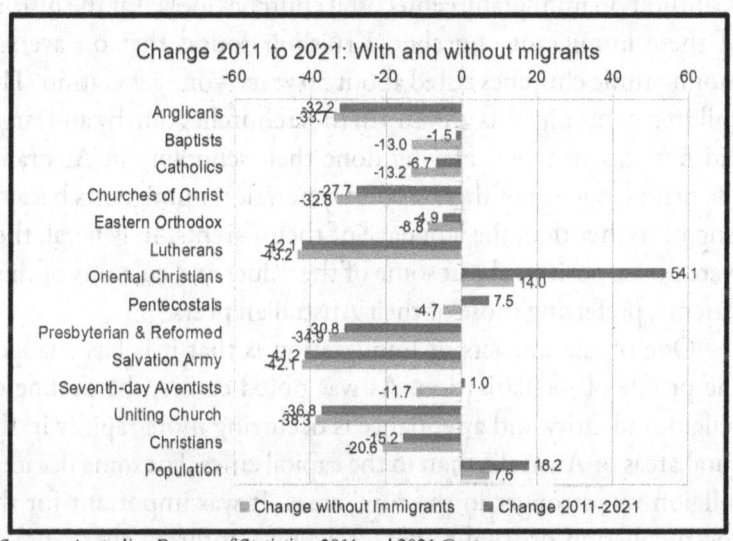

Sources: Australian Bureau of Statistics, 2011 and 2021 Censuses

Figure 2 shows that Baptists actually declined in numbers by just 1.5 per cent between 2011 and 2021, but without immigration, that decline would have been 13 per cent. Pentecostals actually grew by 7.5 per cent, not quite as fast as population growth, but significant all the same. Without immigrants, they would have declined in numbers by 4.7 per cent. Seventh-day Adventists also grew in that decade by 1.0 per cent, but would have declined by 12 per cent without immigrants.

Those denominations which have welcomed comparatively few immigrants over the past years are generally declining much more rapidly than others. Thus, Anglicans, Churches of Christ, Lutherans, Salvation Army and the Uniting Church have all declined very significantly and immigration has made comparatively little difference.

From the point of view of many denominations, it would appear that the immigrants are 'saving' the churches. However, the long-term impact is not as rosy. A 2023 doctoral thesis by Uwe Kruithoff on immigrant Pentecostal churches looked at the history of these immigrant churches. Kruithoff found that on average mono-ethnic churches lasted about 30 years – one generation. The children of immigrants grew up in these churches but, by and large, did not stay in them. Having done their schooling in Australia, the main language of these second generation immigrants became English rather than the language of their parents. In general, they were not as positive about some of the values and customs of their parents, preferring those of their Australian peers.

One of the impacts of immigration is that it is has changed the profile of secularisation. As was noted earlier, the decline of religious identity and attendance is occurring more rapidly in the rural areas of Australia than in the capital cities. For some decades, religion was stronger in the rural areas. It was important for the social cohesion of rural towns. Religion reinforced that sense of duty to the community in which all needed to play a part for the survival of the community. It was important for the farming communities which depended on each other's equipment, skills and good will to reap the harvest.

But rural communities have declined in social cohesion. In many places, businesses have bought the family farms and put in farm managers and employees who have little commitment to the community. Farms are larger and more self-sufficient. In many places, improved roads and even access to aircraft has reduced the isolation of farming communities and the interdependence of those communities.

Now religious identity and attendance is declining more in rural communities than in the cities. The biggest factor causing the different patterns in rural and city areas is the fact that the majority of immigrants have settled in the major cities in Australia. It is here that they have been able to find employment. Here they have found people who shared their language, religion and customs.

There was an interesting televised 'experiment' in Maryborough, Victoria, an Australian regional town. The program, shown on SBS television, was called *Meet the Neighbours* and hosted by the TV personality Myf Warhurst. The population of the town was ageing and there were also many people with disabilities in the town. Cheaper housing in such areas often brings in people who are partly or largely dependent on welfare benefits. The human services in the town, such as the aged care home, were struggling to find workers. Even the sports club which provided meals could not find people to employ to cook or to serve. So the town advertised for immigrants and offered them cheap accommodation. They welcomed in the people who took up the offer. A range of immigrants, from South America, Africa, India and other places responded and found work in the town. Some of them organised community activities which represented their culture: their food, their music and their dance. These people and the elements of culture they introduced were generally well accepted. Yet, over the subsequent couple of years, one by one the immigrant families returned to larger population centres where they could mix more easily with their own kith and kin.

Second generation immigrants

The journey into the broader Australian culture is not an easy one for immigrants. There are some who react strongly in a negative way to the Australian culture. They do not like its values and customs. They retreat into their own community, and sometimes lash out in opposition to what they see around them. But the majority of immigrants' children, to varying degrees, feel positively about the world in which they are growing up. Some children of immigrants continue to be involved in the religious communities of their parents, but others do not. The parents often find it hard to understand why their children do not retain their commitment to their language, culture, heritage and religion. In churches of elderly immigrants I have visited, they made excuses for their children: that they were very busy with the responsibilities of work and family. However, one could feel that they were sad that their children were not active in the church community.

Surveys show that about 30 per cent of those immigrants who identify as Christian attend a church monthly or more often, compared with close to 10 per cent of other Australians. That high level of involvement moderates a little over the years as immigrants find their place in the wider Australian community. The level of involvement among second generation immigrants is similar to that of the wider Australian community.

This generalisation about attendance varies from one culture to another. Those cultures which feel very different culturally from the wider Australian culture may spend longer in their own communities. Thus, some Islamic cultures have tight internal structures and it is likely that these cultures will retain their religious communities longer than some Buddhist communities, for example. The Greek community has a strong, proud sense of identity and this has helped retain people over several generations in the Greek Orthodox Church, although Greeks of the second generation are often not as involved in their churches as those of the first generation.

Looking at attendance patterns across the Australian population, close to 50 per cent of all adults in Australia who attend a church monthly or more often are immigrants or members of immigrant families. Immigrants constitute a huge portion of church attenders. As the flows of immigration continue in coming decades, it is likely that some immigrants will continue to find homes within their religious communities and they will continue to give life to those communities. However, there will also be a flow out of the religious communities of second and third generation immigrants as they find their place in the wider Australian society.

The pro-family values of immigrants

One of the reasons for the religiosity of immigrants is that many come from cultures which have the pro-family values discussed in chapter three. Some immigrants come on humanitarian visas. Most of them come from very poor and often oppressed backgrounds, from Africa or from the Middle East or Afghanistan. They come from countries where there are no welfare safety nets and where dependence on the family is of huge importance. For the survival of their societies, having several children has been necessary. Children have been an economic advantage in that, even in their primary school years, they have begun to assist in earning an income. The commitment of those children to care for their parents in their declining years is critical for the wellbeing of the ageing members of the population. Hence, religion has played an important role in reinforcing those values of duty to the family. Personal fulfilment must play a secondary role to the duty to the family.

Apart from those on humanitarian visas, many other immigrants have come to Australia for economic reasons. Even if they were not in poverty, they have come from communities where there were weak social welfare systems and where wages were low. Many of them have come from cultures where the pro-family values protect the family unit and focus on the bearing and raising of children. Thus, they too have valued religion in reinforcing those family values.

Once in Australia, the strangeness of the culture makes the family members dependent on each other. They negotiate their way together in a land where the language and customs are foreign. Religion helps to keep them together.

However, the religious communities become weaker over time. In the 1980s and 1990s, tens of thousands of immigrants arrived from Vietnam. While some were Catholic, the majority were Buddhist. They built many Buddhist temples. However, the longitudinal data obtained from population censuses and released by the Australian Bureau of Statistics showed that between 2006 and 2016 about 100,000 Buddhists had turned to describe themselves as having 'no religion'. The longitudinal data also showed some leakage from the more recent Islamic and Hindu communities. This trend of leakage to 'no religion' from Buddhism, Hinduism and Islam is likely to continue in second and third generation immigrants.

Another trend is that the proportion of immigrants arriving in Australia who come without a religion is increasing. Among immigrants arriving between 1971 and 1976, just 9 per cent had no religion. Among immigrants arriving between 1981 and 1986, it had risen to 20 per cent. A decade later, between 1991 and 1996, it was 25 per cent. Among those who arrived between 2006 and 2016, 30 per cent said they had 'no religion'. Among the more than one million immigrants who arrived in Australia between 2017 and 2021, 28.5 per cent described themselves as having 'no religion'. It was down a little on the previous decade as fewer of these recent immigrants came from Europe. However, the overall trend of increasing numbers of immigrants having 'no religion' is evident. If secularisation is indeed an international process, we can expect that the proportion of immigrants who have no religion will generally increase, although the patterns will vary depending on where immigrants are coming from. The overall effect, however, will be that immigration will have less impact on the growth of religion in Australia in the future. Thus, the extent to which immigration will slow the rate of secularisation will itself slow, though this may take several generations.

In summary

Immigration is slowing down the rate of secularisation in Australia at the present time. Most immigrants come from societies where the duty to the family is necessary for survival and where religion has played a major role in reinforcing that sense of duty. Religious communities in Australia have welcomed immigrants and helped them to meet people with the same language and cultural values as themselves. They have provided opportunities for immigrants to educate their children in their language and in those cultural and religious traditions. Christian communities as well as those of other religions have benefitted immensely from the influx of immigrants. Interestingly, that influx of immigrants into the major cities has meant that, recently, the decline of the churches in rural and regional Australia has been greater than in the major cities.

However, the importance of the religious communities fades particularly in the second and third generation of immigrants as they find their place in the wider Australian culture. Their involvement in those religious communities declines to a similar level of involvement as others in the wider community. It is also likely that the long-term impact of immigration on the growth of the religious communities will slow. With secularisation happening world-wide, it is likely that more future immigrants will describe themselves as having 'no religion'.

CHAPTER 6

WHY SOME DENOMINATIONS ARE DECLINING FASTER THAN OTHERS

Why are the most tolerant churches declining most rapidly?

In chapters three and four, it was argued that a major factor in the current rapid decline in religious identification and attendance is the change in values. As people focus on personal fulfilment they find themselves in conflict with the traditional religious values of duty to family and community. The tolerance of diversity which allows them to pursue personal fulfilment conflicts with the conformity and obedience which is expected in most religious communities.

Yet, the more progressive Christian communities are the ones which appear to be declining most rapidly. Those denominations which are tolerant of diversity and which are least demanding of conformity and obedience are declining more rapidly than more conservative denominations. The Uniting Church, which is probably most tolerant of diversity and progressive in its social policies, is declining more rapidly than most other denominations.

Conservative denominations have argued that the difference in the rates of decline has to do with theology. In their view, those who are committed to the truth of the Bible will continue to maintain the tradition while those who have, what they see as, a wishy-washy theology which allows in all kinds of un-Biblical ideas will fail. However, the truth is more complex.

In their book *That was the Church That Was: How the Church of England Lost the English People*, the British commentators Andrew Brown and Linda Woodhead showed very clearly how the evangelical sector of the Church of England organised itself very well and became the dominant sector. At the same time, however, with their conservative theology, they lost the connection with the general population in England. There are strong parallels with what has happened in Australia. In many parts of Australia, the evangelical Anglican churches with their clear Biblical theology have become dominant, threatening the very survival of the Anglo-Catholics and even the broad centrist Anglicans as Muriel Porter has well described in her book *A New Exile? The future of Anglicanism*. They have been well organised in planting churches and have actively advocated for their faith. Yet, these evangelical churches have resisted the idea of the equality of males and females in church leadership and have promoted the idea of male headship in the home. In general, they have been more authoritarian in style and less tolerant of diversity than the broad Anglican churches. So why have they become so dominant, given their conflict with the dominant social values?

A similar story may be told of other evangelical denominations such as the continuing Presbyterians. The one-third of Presbyterians who decided not to join with The Uniting Church have evolved into a very different church from what constituted Presbyterianism before the union in 1977. They back-tracked on women's ordination and no longer allowed women to be ordained to lead as ministers. They have pursued a much more conservative agenda in terms of attitudes to sexuality than The Uniting Church. Yet attendances have grown in some Presbyterian churches compared to a more widespread decline in The Uniting Church.

Among those denominations which have been growing in numbers in recent years, even if they have not grown as a percentage of the population, are the Baptists, the Pentecostals, and the

Seventh-day Adventists. These groups are quite different in their theology from each other. Most Baptists can be described as being evangelical, focusing on the authority of the Bible. The Pentecostals also have strong views about the authority of the Bible and in many ways are similar to the evangelicals. However, they add to that the authority and experience of the Holy Spirit through personal experience, commonly expressed in speaking in tongues. The Seventh-day Adventists are also similar to the evangelicals in many respects, but add to that some emphases from their founder, Ellen White. They emphasise physical health and diet with a general prohibition of drugs of all kinds, including caffeine and alcohol.

The other groups which are growing are the Eastern Orthodox, and even more, the Oriental Orthodox. Both have grown through recent immigration and are associated with specific ethnic identities. They are also distinct in their strict adherence to ancient liturgies and generally have conservative approaches to social values.

The Catholic Church has male priests only and has conservative values centred on family life. It has been slow to allow divorced people who have remarried to fully partake in the church's activity. The Catholic Church continues to prohibit the use of the contraceptive pill, even by married couples, although, in practice, this teaching is widely ignored. The Catholic Church also strongly opposes abortion. At the same time, there has been more sexual abuse of children by clergy in the Catholic Church than in any other denomination. Yet, more people identify with the Catholic Church than any other Christian denomination in Australia, and its population is only slowly declining compared with Anglicans, Lutherans, Salvation Army and Uniting Church. Figure 4 summarises the changes between 2016 and 2021 in the various denominations.

Figure 3. Percentage Change in Membership in Various Denominations between 2016 and 2021

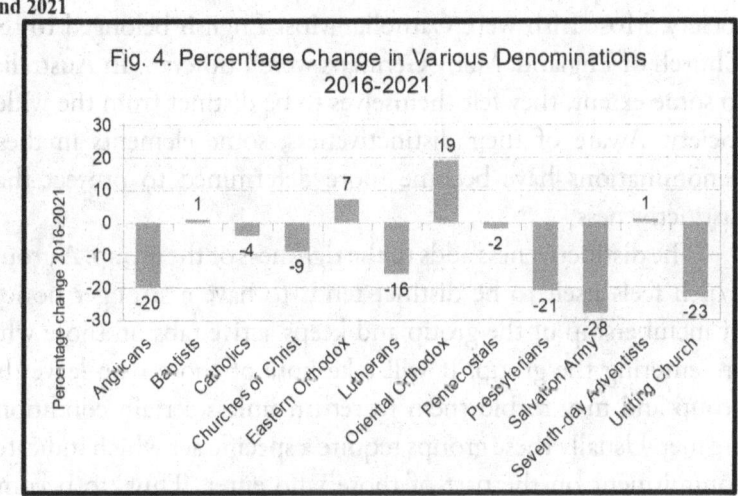

Source: Australian Bureau of Statistics, Censuses 2016 and 2021.

Distinctness from society

We noted in the last chapter that those ethnic groups which have seen themselves as most distinct from the people around them have tended to keep their identity longer. Thus, Islam is not declining as rapidly as Buddhism, for example, because Buddhism has not emphasised its distinctiveness from the Western world as much as Islam has. So the same principle applies to people who identify with particular Christian denominations. Those people who feel most strongly that they are very different from those who live around them and from the wider culture in general are most likely to maintain that identity and to pass on that sense of distinctiveness to their children. Thus, these groups have maintained their numbers over a longer period.

There is a distinction between those groups which feel very distinct from the rest of society and those groups which do not. In the past, some of these groups have been dominant in society. Most Irish were Catholic. Most English belonged to the Church of England. Many Germans were Lutheran. In Australia, to some extent, they felt themselves to be distinct from the wider society. Aware of their distinctiveness, some elements in these denominations have become more determined to protect that distinctiveness.

The distinctiveness adds to the tightness of the group. A group which feels itself to be distinct tends to have a stronger notion of membership of the group and keeps active tabs on those who are entering the group. It will take note of those who leave the group and may forbid them to return unless certain conditions are met. Usually these groups require a specific act which indicates commitment on the part of those who enter. Thus, to become a member of a Baptist Church one usually needs to be baptised as a conscious personal act. Being baptised as an infant is not considered sufficient for membership. Only after adult baptism (which usually means being immersed in a baptistry, a pool, river or sea) can one become a member.

While the decision to be baptised is often referred to by Baptists as conversion, it mostly occurs among the children of those born into Baptist families. Nevertheless, because they offer a distinctively different way of life, these groups which see themselves as different from the wider society do attract those who want a change in life, those who feel life has not been going well for them.

Nevertheless, over time, these groups tend to weaken in their distinctiveness. Members push the boundaries a little. Thus, Baptists, for example, used to strongly discourage all drinking of alcoholic drinks among their members. However, over time, that discouragement is weakened. Thus, there is a general weakening of distinctiveness. This can be seen, for example, in the history of Methodism. It is a story which is told well in *The Churching of America, 1776-1990*, written by the American sociologists. Roger

Finke and Rodney Stark. The Methodists began with a strong emphasis on their 'holiness' and distinctiveness from the wider society. They strongly discouraged the drinking of alcohol and encouraged piety expressed in Bible study and prayer.

Over time, however, these emphases weakened. With members becoming more affluent and having a greater role in society, and with the clergy becoming more educated and more interested in respect in the society, the vigour of the original movement was lost. Their focus turned more to doing good works in the wider society than their personal piety. In Australia, they had lost most of that vigour and sense of distinctiveness that was associated with an emphasis on holiness before the formation of The Uniting Church in Australia into which they moved as a whole denomination in 1977.

Finke and Stark also argued in *The Churching of America, 1776-1990* that ecumenical movements generally fail. The more open denominations are to ecumenism, the weaker their growth. They argue that where denominations compete with each other and emphasise their differences, they are most likely to grow. When they seek to merge and minimise differences, they lose their vigour which leads to decline. While I do not agree with Finke and Stark that secularisation occurs when religious groups fail to compete with each other, I do think that an emphasis on distinctiveness from the world has helped to maintain numbers in some denominations. At the same time, Finke and Stark fail to recognise that those groups which place most emphasis on their distinctiveness generally remain small and unable to attract large numbers of people from mainstream society.

People involved in Protestant churches tend to move freely between churches of different denominations. There is some movement from the more conservative groups to the more progressive groups. People may feel more comfortable in groups which fit more broadly with the general values of the population.

Other people move the other way: into groups which offer the more distinct boundaries and stronger values. These groups offer great security and a more distinctive way of life. At the same time, people in them are more likely to feel that they are in the 'truth'.

With their sense of distinctiveness, these groups which see themselves as distinct from society take great care to provide social opportunities for their members. They have social times for the whole group. Many of them make much more use of small groups such as Bible study and prayer groups which meet during the week. There is less time, then, and less need, for their members to be involved in the wider society which may 'corrupt' them.

Holding that distinctiveness also means that they are often more authoritarian in their leadership. In this way, they emphasise their distinctiveness and what it is that they feel makes them 'true' to the faith they hold. Their leaders emphasise their distinctiveness and are loathe to enter into discussion on areas where their distinctiveness might be questioned.

These groups often have distinctive organisations which cover a great range of the aspects of life. Thus, many have their own schools, their own hospitals and their own aged care homes. It is easy to spend one's whole life in Catholic organisations, for example. Around 55 per cent of Catholic children go to Catholic schools. There is also the possibility of going to a Catholic university. One can work in Catholic hospitals, aged care homes, welfare organisations, or in the educational institutions, and complete one's life-cycle in a Catholic aged-care home. Until recently there was a Catholic insurance company. Thus, many Catholics can live almost their whole lives in Catholic contexts, from primary school to aged care centre. The Catholics, partly because of their size in Australia, have done this more than most groups. More than 3,000 Catholic organisations employ a total of 220,000 people in Australia, second only to the number employed by the Commonwealth government. This distinctive identity has contributed to the fact that the numbers of people identifying as Catholic have not declined as much as the Anglicans and Uniting Church, for example.

Denominations may also run other industries. The Seventh-day Adventists have their own food-making companies such as Sanitarium which makes breakfast cereals. Within these organisations, they are able to employ many of their own members.

The result of having a range of distinctive organisations associated with a denomination is that many of their members live within their own organisations for much of their lives. They are continuously surrounded by people who believe in similar things and hold similar values. Very often, it means that they are reminded – perhaps even on a daily basis – by rituals which make them feel distinct.

It is noteworthy that while identity as Catholic has not fallen as quickly as in many other denominations, church attendance has declined more sharply in Catholic Churches in Australia. In 1989, surveys indicated that 29 per cent of Catholics were attending Mass weekly, meaning that the total attendance was around 1.3 million. A report by the National Centre for Pastoral Research of the official Mass count of the Catholic Church in 2021 found that 417,350 people attended Mass on a typical week-end representing 8.2 per cent of those who identified as Catholic in the 2021 Census. While people still call themselves Catholic and may continue to be involved in Catholic schools, hospitals, aged care homes and other Catholic organisations, many no longer go to Mass. Many have lost confidence in the church and in the clergy.

In their attempt to hold members and be responsive to them, many conservative denominations have been adaptive in their means of communication. They have been responsive to contemporary music tastes and make much use of contemporary bands and songs. They have adapted their buildings using screens, projectors, and LCD screens. Apart from the Catholics and the

Orthodox, their leaders usually dress in contemporary forms of business dress when leading services.

They vary in local autonomy. Baptist Churches are quite autonomous locally. This has allowed them to adapt to the local community ... or in other cases, as autonomous communities, fail to adapt to the contexts. Seventh-day Adventist Churches are more centrally organised, but as a small and well-organised denomination, they have adapted.

While those denominations which see themselves as highly distinct from the wider society have conservative values, they have worked hard to establish boundaries with the wider society. Through their schools and other institutions, they have sought to bring up their children within the group and have discouraged engagement with the wider society. As a result, they have maintained their numbers better than the more progressive denominations. However, these more exclusive denominations have not attracted many people to join them and all of them would be experiencing some decline if it were not for the immigrants who are boosting their numbers.

The charismatic revival

In the 1970s, a movement emerged that challenged the idea of secularisation. The movement had its roots in a number of churches which started in the first decade of the 20th century, in the United States, South Africa, Australia and England. It was a movement which emphasised the experience of the Holy Spirit in one's personal life – an experience which was accompanied by fainting, speaking in tongues (strange languages or in sounds not recognisable as human language), in uncontrollable laughing. The movement was formed outside existing churches, and, in the early days, often under the leadership of women. Rallies were held and music with a strong beat and repetitive words were used to build the emotional tone. The speakers focused on emotional calls to change one's life. People came forward to receive blessings and prayers which were often accompanied by these deep personal experiences which were seen as being 'filled with the Holy Spirit'. While these rallies attracted people's curiosity, the churches which emerged in the first two-thirds of the twentieth century remained small.

Then, suddenly, in the 1970s, the movement took off in many parts of the world. Thousands of Pentecostal churches were formed and they were quickly filled with young, enthusiastic people. They were going to change the world, bringing the experience of God into everyday life.

One of the largest mega churches in Melbourne, a product of the Pentecostal and charismatic movement which began in the 1970s.

These new churches had the great advantage that they could be different. It was not the case of trying to change the old and staid ways of doing things. They did not build especially elaborate churches, but rather they were happy using school halls and warehouses. In countries such as England and Australia, where large numbers of people purchased their own cars in the 1960s and 1970s, people were no longer tied to walking or catching infrequent public transport. Thus, Pentecostals built churches without attention to local suburban boundaries. People were attracted to those Pentecostal churches which were most professionally run and offered the best music and speakers. Thus, some of the Pentecostal churches grew into great mega-churches with thousands of attenders. However, many other Pentecostal churches remained small and struggling.

The movement attracted intense interest from people in other denominations. Some leaders in Anglican, Catholic, Baptist and many other denominations adopted the songs and the style of music. The preachers tried to copy some of the emotionally charged patterns of the Pentecostal pastors. And in some of these churches, the emotional expressions of faith such as speaking in tongues broke out. This became known as the Charismatic movement, based on the Greek word for 'gifts' that was used to describe the gifts of the Holy Spirit.

The movement adopted some features of evangelical churches. Most tended to be literal in their interpretation of the Bible and authoritative in the ways in which they presented it. They adopted the conservative social values of the evangelicals with an emphasis on the family and the rejection of sexual expression outside marriage. While women had played a major role in the rise of the movement, by the 1970s, women were discouraged from taking leadership positions in some of their churches. Nevertheless, many people from more staid and conservative churches were attracted by the experientialism and enthusiasm of this movement and also by its conservative, family-centred values.

Within a period of just forty years, the Pentecostal churches grew more than the churches of any other denomination in Australia. In 2024, the Australian Christian Churches, the largest of the Pentecostal denominations in Australia, claimed on its website to have 350,000 constituents. In 2021, in *Australia's Religious and Non-Religious Profiles*, I estimated from surveys that the monthly attendance of Pentecostals was around 300,000, second in size only to the Catholic churches with around 420,000. I estimated that Anglicans had about 280,000 and Baptists around 240,000 people attending monthly or more often, with a little under 100,000 attending Uniting Churches.

Yet, as Brown and Woodhead noted in *That Was the Church That Was*, experiential movements such as this need constant renewal. There is a need for new experiences. At the same time, there have been some scandals in some of the largest and most successful churches of both a financial and sexual kind which have resulted in tens of thousands of attenders leaving the church. Tensions have also emerged in the movement over the roles of women in leadership and the teaching about gender roles in the home.

Research for a doctoral thesis by Mark Bohr, a former Pentecostal pastor, indicated that many young people growing up in Pentecostal churches were leaving because of the authoritarianism of the churches and the lack of debate about issues such as same-sex marriage. While there had been continuous growth since the start of the movement in the early 20th century, the 2021 Census showed that the numbers of people identifying themselves as Pentecostal or with a Pentecostal denomination had declined from the previous Census in 2016.

One of the problems with groups that are highly distinct from the wider society is that they can never attract the majority of people, or even a large minority. As they attract people, they tend to weaken the expectations they have of their members. But then, as they weaken, break-away groups claim they are preserving the purity of the original group.

Possibly as many as half of all the people who attend a church in Australia at least monthly today are Pentecostals or in a church which has been influenced by the charismatic or evangelical movements. The other half are mostly in churches which also carry an ethnic or national heritage as well as a faith component. Both of these groups place great importance on their distinctiveness from the wider society.

On the other hand, some of the distinctive characteristics of the Pentecostals are weakening. In the large Pentecostal mega-churches, it has become less common for people to speak in tongues, for example. While the Pentecostal churches attract some people from the wider society who feel that the very different way of life and values that these groups hold could be attractive, they are also losing people who are frustrated by the intolerance and authoritarianism among some leaders and the lack of gender equality in the churches.

The decline of the progressive churches

The number of people attending broad and progressive churches has declined much more than among those churches which value their distinctiveness. Immediately after World War II, the 1947 Census showed that almost 40 per cent of the population saw themselves as Anglican (or Church of England) and 22 per cent saw themselves as Presbyterian or Methodist. These were the mainstream churches and were central to society.

Over the years since 1947, both denominations have shrunk very considerably. In 2021, just 10 per cent of the population saw themselves as Anglican and 4 per cent as Presbyterian or Uniting Church (with The Uniting Church having absorbed the Methodists apart from a few small break-away movements). In both the Anglican and Uniting denominations, there are some churches influenced by the evangelical and charismatic movements and these tend to be larger churches.

The major reason for the decline in numbers is that many children growing up in these denominations have not felt that it was necessary to stay involved in the churches. While being more progressive, they were a little slow in some cases to keep up with the changes in the population. The predecessors to The Uniting Church began ordaining women into leadership before the Union in 1977, but male leadership continued to dominate until into the 1990s. Some parts of the Anglican Church ordained female leaders in the 1980s, but there is still only one female bishop in Australia who has full responsibility for a diocese, although there are some female auxiliary bishops.

One suspects that as young couples moved in with each other and sex prior to marriage became the norm, many of these people did not feel quite at home in the churches. This was not what these churches had traditionally taught, even if they made little fuss about it compared with the more conservative churches.

The progressive churches have encouraged people to think for themselves. With the freedom not to take the Bible literally, many people raised in progressive churches have come to the conclusion that the Christian faith does not make much sense to them. They no longer believe in a God who came to earth in the form of a man, Jesus. They are not sure about life after death. Even if the church does not require adherence to particular doctrines, these people have found no need to stay. With the fading of the importance of religion in many areas of life and awareness that some of the churches values did not accord well with the wider society, people in the more progressive churches have left. While individuals were valued because they were seen as created in the image of God, without that belief, individuals can be still be valued as unique human beings.

As the more progressive people have left the churches, so even the most progressive denominations have become more conservative. It is not a result of a change of the theology of the people within them. Rather, it results from the fact that those who take a conservative line, who see themselves in opposition to the wider world, or distinctive from it, have remained in the churches while the more progressive attenders have left.

The increasing conservatism in the churches was noted in a study of Christianity in Australia by the Rationalist Society. Neil Francis, a researcher in social and medical areas, wrote a report, *Religiosity in Australia*, released in 2022. Francis used the Australian Election Study, research which is conducted by the Australian National University after elections. The 2019 edition of this survey involved random responses from 2,179 voters.

Based on that data, Francis argued that those who attend a church monthly or more often tended to align themselves with Coalition agendas. While a few attenders aligned themselves with the Greens, the proportion of church attenders aligning themselves with Labor had declined. However, his observation that most attenders take a conservative stance politically as well as on social values is affirmed by other surveys such as the *Australian Survey of Social Attitudes*.

On the other hand, Francis correctly pointed out that many church attenders do support abortion, marriage equality, voluntary assisted dying and the decriminalisation of marijuana. The Australian Christian Lobby and many church leaders who speak out on social issues do not speak for most people who identify themselves as Christian, nor even those who attend churches. Nevertheless, overall, church attenders take more conservative positions on these issues as well as in their political voting than have church attenders in the past.

Just one interesting impact of this more conservative approach can be seen in the numbers of children born to women who continue to identify with a religion. Many of these people place great importance on family life and on having children and see women's primary role in child-bearing and child-raising. As shown in Figure 4, a comparatively high proportion have three or more children compared with those women who describe themselves as having no religion. It seems likely that these people who have continued to identify have found confirmation in their religious beliefs for the importance they give to family life.

Figure 4. The Proportion of Women 15 to 50 with Three or More Children by Religious Group

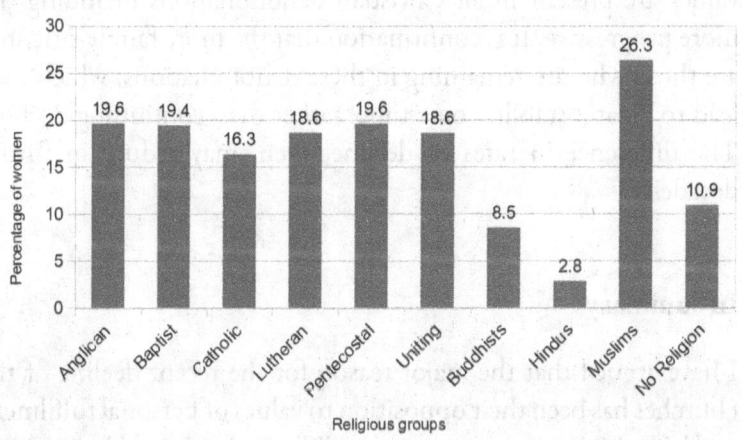

Source: Australian Census, 2021.

People participate in church as they feel comfortable with the values. Even the more progressive denominations continue to reinforce the values of family life. They do so through their emphasis on marriage and through the ways in which they assist families to socialise their children. It is interesting that the proportion of women with three or more children shown in Figure 4 varies little from one denomination to another. The Catholics who have, in the past, encouraged large families now have slightly smaller families than the Protestants. It is interesting that the Buddhists have smaller families. This may reflect the fact that Buddhism, as a religion, does not emphasise family life as much as other religions. The proportion of Hindus with three or more children is smaller again. The size of the Hindu families may reflect the very recent arrival of many Hindus into Australia with a higher proportion of them being younger women. Women who identify as Islamic are more likely than any other group to have three or more children, reflecting their strong orientation to the family-oriented values.

Figure 4 is slim evidence, but it suggests that the family-oriented values are present in all Christian denominations including the more progressive. It is confirmation that the more family-oriented are those who are remaining in these denominations, which may lead to greater stability over time, rather than continuing decline. The difference in rates of decline, then, may reduce in future decades.

In summary

I have argued that the major reason for the recent decline of the churches has been their opposition to values of personal fulfilment and how this has been expressed in different forms of relationships, and in the importance given to tolerance and equity in society. Yet, the denominations which have most espoused tolerance and equity and have not expected conformity and obedience have been declining most rapidly. The conservative denominations which have emphasised distinctiveness from society have tended to maintain their numbers more strongly than the more progressive denominations. Historical studies show that denominations, such as the Methodists, have often begun with a strong sense of their distinctiveness and with rapid growth. As their distinctiveness has weakened, so have their rates of growth and this is now apparent in the Pentecostal churches in Australia which grew very strongly between 1970 and 2000.

Progressive churches have declined because people no longer see a reason to attend. Many of those who have grown up in the more progressive churches have questioned both the beliefs and values of the churches. Frequently they have simply felt that there was no need to attend church: they could live out their values in society without reference to the church. This includes those who have seen the churches quite in step with their own values and attitudes.

As people with more progressive views have left the churches, the result has been that all denominations have become more conservative. The people who have remained, even in the more progressive denominations, have been those who have valued the emphasis on family values. The 2021 Census has shown they have significantly larger families than people of no religion! It is possible that as a consequence of the persistence of these more conservative values in the progressive churches, their rates of decline will slow.

CHAPTER 7

HOW PEOPLE FIND MEANING TODAY

In the past, religion has been a major source of meaning for most human beings. The only major exception to that has been in communist countries where communism has performed as a quasi-religion: giving people a sense of how the world works and how people have a place within it. In chapter three, I explored how religion had given people a set of values to live by, rooted primarily in duty towards family and community. We saw how these values had changed in times of peace and economic boom and in the context of low infant mortality and strong welfare systems. Personal fulfilment had taken the place of family and national duties. In this chapter, I will explore further how people are finding a meaning and purpose for their lives in a post-religious world.

Beyond religion

While church attendance and belief have declined, many people throughout the Western world continue to believe that there *may* be a God, and that God may help us if we need it. They feel that if there is a God, then God would be benevolent and would be accessible outside the rules and structures of organised religion.

In a 2005 book on the religiosity of American youth, *Soul Searching*, Christian Smith and Melinda Denton argued that the belief of most young people in America could be summarised as 'moral therapeutic deism'. By 'deism', Smith and Denton were summarising the fact that most young people believed there was some sort of God. 'Therapeutic' referred to the idea that they believed God would help people when they needed it. 'Moral' refers to the fact that most people believed that God wanted people to be 'good' in a moral sense. Similar patterns were found in studies of youth culture in Australia. These studies were conducted by the Christian Research Association along with researchers from the Australian Catholic University and Monash University, and reported in *The Spirit of Generation Y: Young people's spirituality in a changing Australia (2007) and Putting Life Together: Findings from Australian Youth Spirituality Research*, (2007).

Many young people thought there might be a God, but had little sense of what God might be like except the general sense that God would be kind and helpful. Young people, doubtful about the existence of God, prayed when they felt they needed extra help, because, they said, "you never know, it might work". What we also noted, however, was that there was less emphasis on the requirement for moral behaviour. It seems likely that this pattern exists broadly across the Australian public, although we must add that the significance of God has faded markedly since this research in 2007. Fewer people would even think to pray today than in 2007.

But 'moral therapeutic deism' is not the sort of religious faith that is relevant to the whole of life. It is more like belief in Father Christmas, who will give presents at Christmas to children who have been good. It is more like a superstitious 'add-on' to the framework and values which rule the patterns of everyday life. It is not a way of thinking about life as a whole. In our study of youth culture, we came to the conclusion that the most important thing in life to most young people was personal fulfilment in the form of family, friends and fun. Again, this is also the dominant pattern among most adults. Many people would see personal fulfilment in terms of family, friends and fun, although others would add more to that as we shall note later.

For 85 per cent of Australians, and similar proportions in the United Kingdom and northern Europe, religious faith has largely faded in everyday life. They no longer attend a church frequently. They no longer engage in regular prayer or other religious rituals. Beliefs are vague and even if they think there may be a God, the idea has little influence on how they live their lives, except perhaps as an additional resource in a crisis. Some people have suggested that the rising notion is that of being 'spiritual' rather than being 'religious'. Let us look at that.

Spiritual but not religious

The first major study in Australia of being 'spiritual but not religious' was conducted in 2002 through a national survey, the results of which were published in *Spirit Matters*, a book by Kaldor, Hughes and Black (2010). Having analysed responses to a number of questions, 17 per cent of the adult Australian population were classified by the researchers as 'spiritual' rather than religious. At that point, two types of spirituality were identified. The first was eclectic with people drawing on a range of religious resources rather than being committed to one religion. Some of these people also drew on New Age ideas and resources. The second type of spirituality was based around a connection to land or to nature. Their spirituality was experienced in oneness with nature and was often accompanied by a commitment to the care of nature.

Since then, it has become common to ask people in surveys whether they were religious and spiritual, religious but not spiritual, spiritual but not religious, or neither religious nor spiritual. In the 2018 *Australian Survey of Social Attitudes*, 24 per cent of Australians responded that they were 'spiritual but not religious'. An additional 18 per cent described themselves as both spiritual and religious and 14 per cent said they were religious but not spiritual. The *Contributing to Australian Society* survey, conducted by the Christian Research Association in 2016, reported 25 per cent of Australians as 'spiritual but not religious'. An additional 21 per cent of the population described themselves as 'religious and spiritual'. Fourteen per cent said they were religious but not spiritual. In both surveys more than 40 per cent of Australians describes themselves as 'spiritual' with between 32 and 35 per cent affirming the word 'religious'. The word 'religion' has become less popular than the word 'spiritual' for Australian adults to describe themselves.

But what does it mean to describe oneself as 'spiritual' and particularly as 'spiritual but not religious'? Some people such as the British sociologists Heelas and Woodhead have argued that we are not moving into a secular era, but rather a 'spiritual' era, in which spirituality rather than secularism is replacing religion. Other sociologists, such as David Voas and Steve Bruce, do not agree and argue that the development of these forms of spirituality is simply a step on the path to secularity.

The proportion of Australians who have chosen the term 'spiritual but not religious' has not grown significantly since 2009. The description was a little more popular with older people than younger people, suggesting the numbers may fall in the future. The 2016 *Contributing to Australian Society* survey found that approximately 75 per cent of those who described themselves as 'spiritual but not religious' used to attend a church, at least during their childhood. Just three per cent of them attended frequently at the time of the survey, and another 13 per cent attended a church occasionally. This suggests that many of these people may be affirming some dimensions of the religiosity that was important to them in their early years, but rejecting institutional religion. The term 'spirituality' is more popular with people with an Australian or northern European background rather than an Asian or Islander background and, for many people, seems to be a way of indicating their rejection of religion, but not all of the values associated with religion.

But there is another reason why some people are willing to affirm the phrase 'spiritual but not religious' while others are not. It is possible that the spiritual may have different value orientations to the 'neither spiritual nor religious'. As noted in chapter three, there is a distinction between the business and knowledge (or people-oriented) class. The business class had values which revolved around self-enhancement, and around the measurable goals in terms of production and economic success. The knowledge class measured success in the incremental development in people's wellbeing, in their education or in their health, for example. Those people whose values focus on people's wellbeing are more likely to use the term 'spiritual' to describe themselves.

A question in the *Contributing to Australian Society* survey in 2016 was about what made life worthwhile for the respondent. The results provide an interesting picture of the values of three groups in Australian society, as shown in Table 5.

Most respondents in each of the three groups reported that family and friends were most important in making life worthwhile. However, those who identified themselves as 'spiritual but not religious' rated being in nature, music and cooking or craft more highly than either the religious or the non-religious. The spiritual but not religious also rated doing things for others, volunteering and participation in community, much higher than did those who said they were neither spiritual nor religious. They place greater importance on the value of caring for others. Those who were neither religious nor spiritual rated their paid work, travel and watching films and television higher than the other groups.

Table 5. Priorities in What Makes Life Worthwhile for Australian Adults by Whether People Described Themselves as Religious, Spiritual or Neither.

Priorities	Religious	Spiritual but not religious	Neither spiritual nor religious
1	Family	Family	Family
2	Religious faith	Friends	Friends
3	Friends	Time in nature	Paid work
4	Volunteering	Doing things for others	Travel
5	Doing things for others	Music	Music
6	Time in nature	Travel	Time in nature
7	Paid work	Volunteering	Doing things for others
8	Music	Paid work	Watching films / TV
9	Travel	Cooking or craft work	Volunteering
10	Participation in community	Participation in community	Cooking or craft work
11	Cooking or craft work	Watching films / TV	Sport
12	Watching films / TV	Sport	Participation in community
13	Sport	Religious faith	Religious faith

Source: *Contributing to Australian Society Survey*, 2016.

These value orientations may arise in different personality types. Low levels of psychoticism, which is associated with higher levels of tendermindedness, for example, have been found to be related to an openness to spirituality. The socialisation of children through the home environment, school and friends also has an impact. The cultural environment also plays a role. For example, it was clear in the Australian study of values that people who had lived through the depression and World War II were more likely to place greater importance on order in life and society, while those who grew up in the relative affluence and peace of the 1970s gave more importance to the values of social wellbeing.

The notion of 'spiritual but not religious' has been criticised for its vagueness. People mean different things when they describe themselves as 'spiritual'. At one level, the notion of being 'spiritual but not religious' is identified more precisely by its negative assertions rather than positive assertions. For many, the phrase is a protest against religion. Many of these people have rejected religion, particularly in its institutional forms. The surveys show that their confidence in religious organisations is very low with just 6 per cent expressing a fair degree of confidence in religious organisations compared with 44 per cent of the religious. They object to the idea of clericalism, of a certain group of people being identified as mediators of the sacred. They object to the notion of creeds and doctrines as the basis of their spirituality. They want tolerance and openness and are strongly affirming of multiculturalism.

The *Contributing to Australian Society* survey (2016) found that just 11 per cent of those who identified themselves as 'spiritual but not religious' affirmed the idea of a god who is external to us and is concerned with human beings. Many of them do believe there are spiritual forces in the universe. Many of them affirm the idea that there is a Mystery at the heart of the universe, but are not convinced about the Christian concept of God.

Looking at the stars, human beings are more aware than ever of the great mysteries of the universe.

As we look at the natural world, we are amazed as its beauty and its complexity. Given what we now know about the stars, some people find it hard to look at them and see their creator encapsulated in metaphors of a human being such as father or king who somehow reaches out to individuals and helps them as they need assistance. In the past, it has been easy to imagine God using human metaphors. But as our conception of the universe has grown, so must our conception of whatever is behind the existence and form of the universe.

We know that there are still great mysteries in the universe. We do not understand the dark matter which – it has been hypothesised – fills much of space. We do not know what happened before the Big Bang and what may have initiated it. Is it possible that there are parallel universes? And why does the universe operate in regular ways, as if governed by laws, rather than being a place of chaos? Whatever is behind the existence of the universe is Mystery.

Others would see the spiritual as something deep within us, rather than as something external to us. In a different way, what is in us as human beings is also Mystery. As we delve into the human psyche, as we reflect deeply on ourselves, on our deepest experiences, we also arrive at Mystery. Apart from all our activity and purpose, apart even from our social relationships, there are times when most human beings find it important to stop and contemplate, to be simply in the moment, to feel the enormity of the university and the beauty of nature.

Drawing on a range of research, Antoon Geels, Professor at Lund University in Sweden, has identified a number of differences between traditional forms of religion and the new forms of spirituality, in that the latter promote:

1. Acceptance of eclectic sources rather than a particular historical tradition;
2. Emphasis on experience rather than on dogma;

3. Focus on the personal rather than the collective;
4. A life-view that is egalitarian rather than hierarchical;
5. Emphasis on the anthropological dimension of life, such as individual growth and wellbeing, rather than the theological; and,
6. A focus on this-worldliness rather than life after death.

He suggested that the first four are all consonant with globalisation, with living in a world where many traditions are recognised and where it is necessary to find ways of living together in a pluralistic environment. The second, third, fifth and sixth points arise out of the emphasis on personal experience.

At the same time as being a protest against religion, the notion of 'spiritual but not religious' is a protest against materialism and placing value on the accumulation of material goods. It is noteworthy that in the *Contributing to Australian Society* survey, those who said they were spiritual but not religious placed volunteering and paid work at a similar level in their priorities for making life worthwhile, while those who were neither religious nor spiritual put paid work much higher. The spiritual but not religious see the most important things in life as relationships and beauty in nature, music and art rather than the sorts of goods which can be purchased in shops. Most would hold an account of reality in which there are dimensions of life which cannot be reduced to chemical and physical forces. Achievement is not measured in money and products but in the wellbeing of the individual and in the depth of relationships.

It has been suggested that some aspects of the thinking of this group go back to elements in Christian heritage that have been lost. Jesus himself often acted in anti-institutional ways and opposed the clericalism of his time. There was an early respect for the natural world, which comes to the fore, for example, in early Celtic

Christian thinking. There is a sense of respect for the wholeness of nature and the indivisibility of life.

Having identified the characteristics of contemporary spirituality noted above, Geels argued that the fundamental traits of the new spiritualities of life are in harmony with the great mystical and spiritual traditions within world religions. He noted that mystics have always drawn attention to a God who is 'Mystery' hidden as well as revealed. In seeking God, the mystics have relied on their own personal experience of that Mystery, which they have often seen as immanent in creation. They have argued that the divine Mystery cannot be limited by dogma and transcends any particular institutional formulation or historical tradition. Their emphasis has often been on union with the divine Mystery in the here and now.

Just as many mystics have stood outside or at the fringes of religious institutions, most people who identify themselves as 'spiritual but not religious' are unlikely to return to a church, or anything like it. Most people who are 'spiritual but not religious' are not interested in any form of organisational structure, especially those that may seek to confine their behaviour by expecting attendance at regular gatherings or by requiring adherence to a set of rules or beliefs. They will not enter into hierarchical organisations in which they are expected to allow the organisation to define what they should believe and how they should live.

Some scholars, such as David Voas and Steve Bruce (2007) in the UK, have argued that the rise of the 'spiritual but not religious' is part of a general movement away from religion into secularism. Many of these people act in secular ways and, in time, will drop all reference to the spiritual. In some respects, 'spirituality' is being reduced to secular forms, and some scholars such as Carrette and King (2005) have suggested that this is ultimately a consumer-driven way of turning what was religious into something 'marketable' to the individual.

The protests against both consumerism and religion may remain, but the distinctiveness of this group may not. These people look for resources which nurture their spirit. They find those resources in nature, often in meditation and forms of contemplation, in pilgrimage and reflective travel, in music and art, as well as in massages and aromas. Some find nurture through educational programs and philosophical discussions. Some are engaged in social justice and political action.

However, in recent interviews with people about meaning and purpose, no one volunteered the use of the language of spirituality. The 'spiritual but not religious' may be a description people pick out in a survey, but it is not a common term in everyday conversations. Without any specific institutional forms, there is no clear group of people who are 'spiritual but not religious'. Many people who do not use this phrase also value being in nature, and appreciate forms of contemplation, music and art. As Table 5 suggests, people vary in their values and the ways they make sense of life, but mostly the differences are in degree. The values are not opposed to each other, but are differences in emphasis. People vary in the activities in which they engage which gives them a sense of personal wellbeing and personal fulfilment.

Civic religion

Another way of looking at post-religious values is by looking at what people celebrate. There is an annual round of celebrations in which most Australians participate. Embedded in them are basic values. Some of these celebrations have religious roots but have been developed in ways that are meaningful to the non-religious. They have been described as forming the basis of a 'civic' or an 'implicit' religion.

Every year begins with a celebration of the fact that we can start anew. We can put our past behind us. We are grateful for what has occurred in the past, but we can approach the future with hope. In the northern hemisphere, it is close to the time when the sun begins to rise on the horizon, another sign of hope.

On 14th February, romantic love is celebrated on Valentine's Day.

Easter is another major celebration. While it is about the new life of spring in Europe, in some places it also carries poignant reminder of those who are suffering. In Melbourne, Australia, Good Friday is the day for the Royal Children's Hospital major appeal.

ANZAC Day on 25th April originally honoured the soldiers who had served in the Australia and New Zealand Army Corps. However, it has become a day to remember all those who have served in the armed forces of Australia and New Zealand, not only in war but also in peace-keeping operations. The day celebrates the values of bravery and sacrifice for country. It also remembers the mateship and loyalty the soldiers have shown towards each other.

Other celebrations revolve around family such as Mother's Day on the second Sunday in May and Father's Day on the first Sunday in September. These celebrations, as have all our celebrations, been milked by commercial companies. Yet, behind them there is the continuing value of parenthood and family life.

In civic religion, the Christmas myths of Santa and his reindeer eclipse the religious story of the birth of Jesus.

Family life and giving to others is a major theme of Christmas. Christmas is often a time when extended families meet and gifts are exchanged. Many charities have Christmas appeals, encouraging people to think of those who are less fortunate than themselves. Again, one wonders how the commercial Christmas story which is all about Father Christmas relates to the real Christmas story about the nativity. Yet, there is here the idea that giving to others is a good thing.

Some of these civic celebrations have their religious counterparts and arose from religious festivals. Most Australians, whether they are religious or not, celebrate these civic festivals. Through them, some common values are maintained throughout the society.

The sources of meaning

While the notion of spirituality and the celebrations of 'civic religion' give a sense of some people's values in a post-religious world, they do not fully explain how people find a sense of meaning. This is best explained by those who have worked in the psychology of meaning.

Tatjana Schnell is an Austrian psychologist who works in Innsbruck and Oslo. In 2021, she published a book called *The Psychology of Meaning in Life*. She argued that 'meaning in life' is one of the terms we use in evaluating our lives. It is not the same as feeling good or being happy. Reviewing her own research and that of other researchers, she argued that the sense of meaning and purpose has four major dimensions:

1. Orientation or direction expressed through goals and purposes;
2. Coherence in these goals and purposes through which we identify higher goals and see others as subsets of them and avoid conflict between them;
3. Belonging – in which we perceive ourselves as part of a larger whole and have a place in the world;
4. Significance in that we feel that our actions have consequences.

Schnell noted that, in the past and for some people today, religion has helped people find a sense of meaning. It has given people a framework for life in which they have found their goals and purposes and coherence in those. It has also given people a sense of belonging and assured them that, as people created by God, they have a place in a larger whole in which our lives have significance.

However, Schnell suggested that, in the Western world, common ways we find meaning are through caring for our families and in friendships. We find it through creative activities and in our social commitments. We may well think of the general aim of making the world a better place, and seeing our roles through our work or our volunteering as contributing to that goal. On the other hand, much of our lives is geared around our care for our families, through providing a home and food and the other necessities of life.

On the other hand, we can also find meaning in particular personal projects, goals or tasks such as in pursuing our family history, or improving our golf handicap. Our goal may simply be to improve our physical health, or to learn another language.

For some people, the goal may be to enjoy life as much as they can. We may do that through holidays or through walking in the bush, through art or music, or through enjoying sport and parties.

Other researchers have focused on the belonging aspect. While having a sense of identity as a citizen of a nation or as a member of a sporting club may give us some sense of meaning, that sense of meaning is much stronger when it involves relationships with other people. Psychologists such as Gordon Flett who wrote *The Psychology of Mattering: Understanding the Human Need to be Significant* (2016) and Isaac and Ora Prilleltensky who wrote *How People Matter: Why It Affects Health, Happiness, Love, Work and Society*, have focused on those relationships people have in which they feel that they matter to others, and that their contribution is recognised as significant. Much meaning is generated through our social connections and through the feedback that those social connections matter to others.

Many of the projects, goals and tasks noted above become much more meaningful to us when we do them for others or in conjunction with others, and we understand that they are meaningful to those people. We know that the ways we care for others matters to them. Meaning is added to the meal that is prepared when it is shared, and when those who share it appreciated the meal ... and the cook. Meaning is added when we share the family history we have put together with other members of the family for whom it evokes good memories and understanding of family life.

It is true that if we feel that we are serving God, then we may well feel that there is an 'ultimate' dimension to what we are doing. Our projects, goals and tasks take on a meaning within a much larger context than ourselves. Yet, it is not necessary for us to relate our activities to what may be understood as God's desire for us. Knowing that what we are doing contributes to the lives of those around us is sufficient to give us a sense of meaning.

In the 2018 *Australian Survey of Social Attitudes*, 58 per cent of adult Australians affirmed "Life is only meaningful if you provide the meaning yourself". An additional 21 per cent were not sure, but only 21 per cent disagreed with that statement. For the majority of Australians, a sense of meaning is not something that is handed to us or provided to us by religion. It arises through our own personal sense of fulfilment and through our social connections. Through social connections, we form friendships in which occur that flow of 'mattering' to others, and feeling that people 'matter' to us.

For some people, the relationships are not personal or face-to-face. Meaning can be developed as people contribute to a movement or a political party or a charity. It can happen in less personal ways. Certainly, many people do find meaning in the projects that they engage in personally.

Entertainment and having fun can give us meaning for a while. But entertainment is often ephemeral. Its value fades rapidly after the fun time. We can enjoy a movie or a concert, but its meaningfulness is soon forgotten unless, perhaps, it becomes something that we share with others and becomes part of our joint memory and our relationship. It is interesting that in Table 5, watching TV and films was low on the lists of what makes life worthwhile, even though most of us spend quite a lot of time doing such activities.

Some people have a much stronger sense of meaning than others. They have a strong sense of purpose and direction in their lives and greater coherence in the various tasks they set themselves. They vary in the strength of the relationships they have with others through which that sense of belonging and mattering is reinforced.

Meaning in life is not something we often talk about, but its absence can be devastating. When a partner or a child dies, for example, we can feel a great hole in our lives. That which contributed so much to our sense of meaning has been taken away. Or when our health is taken away and we can no longer do the things that we had been doing, we can experience a loss of meaning. For some people, the loss of meaning is experienced in retirement, when we are no longer contributing to society through our paid work.

There is now a great deal of research summarised by Schnell, Flett and Isaac and Ora Prilleltensky which shows that people with a strong sense of meaning cope better with the crises in life. They tend to have a strong sense of self-esteem and find a way through the challenges of life when they occur. They find new ways of connecting with others when existing relationships come to an end, for example, through death.

The sense of meaning can also be strengthened in another way. The language of social capital is used in measuring the strength of relationships throughout a society as outlined in the book *Building Stronger Communities* by Hughes, Kaldor and Black. 'Bonding relationships' which are close and supportive are important for everyone. People also need a range of 'bridging relationships' in which they relate to a variety of people who can provide a range of resources for us or companionship, but who are not people they would depend on in a crisis. At the bridging level of relationships, it is important to have 'cross-cutting ties'. In other words, for the sake of the society, it is important to have social relationships which bridge the gaps created by age, gender, social class and education, race and language. It is only through these relationships across the characteristics that would divide us that there can be social cohesion in society. When society is divided between the rich and poor, between the well-educated and the less educated, between people of different races and religions, there is less trust and society is less productive. We can find a stronger sense of meaning and contribute more to social cohesion when we form relationships which bridge those gaps.

There is an important caveat in this discussion. People can find meaning and significant relationships in ways which are socially destructive. Criminal gangs can have a strong sense of meaning and belonging, but are destructive of the wider society. Indeed, terrorists have an ultimate goal which inspires them and gives them a coherent agenda. Purposes which celebrate death and destruction, which accept violence as a legitimate means and treat others as expendable in the process, are 'deeply disturbed' said William Damon in his book *The Path to Purpose* (2008).

The psychologist Paul Wong has also noted that if personal fulfilment is conceived in a hedonistic way of having fun, enjoying life, and having positive feelings, it can be short-lived. He argued that eudaimonia (a term drawn from the Greek philosopher, Aristotle, meaning the highest human good for which humans can strive) was having meaning and purpose plus virtue and inner goodness. Such purpose was visible, he said, in people willing to put the wellbeing of others first, willing to put their community or even the whole of humanity before their own pleasure. The person with eudainomic purpose would not give up in the face of adversity, and could find meaning even in the face of suffering.

In summary

Beyond religion, many people still think there *may* be a God. If so, they imagine that God would be benevolent and helpful. However, this sort of thinking tends to see 'God' as a resource that they might turn to for help in times of need. It is hardly a 'religious faith' which influences how they live.

Close to one quarter of the Australian population describe themselves in surveys as being 'spiritual but not religious'. That phrase often denotes a rejection of institutionalised religion, but it also is indicative that people are not content with a materialistic or mechanistic view of the universe. While the phrase is used by many people who once attended churches, it is also used more by those see the major value in people and relationships rather than in money and products. There is a tendency for these people to place more value than do the non-religious in being in nature, in music and art. However, the group is not very distinct and many people who do not use the language of spirituality have similar values.

Most Australians participate in a series of celebrations through the year. They begin the celebrations on New Year's Day as they embrace the hope of a new beginning. The celebrations include Easter and Christmas which have their secular expressions alongside the religious traditions. They also involve the celebration of romantic love, parenthood and family life.

Psychologists such as Tatjana Schnell have shown how meaning in life is found in coherent directions, goals and purposes, in belonging and significance. Such meaning can be found in the personal project, in hobbies and careers, in social action and personal ambitions. But it is often amplified and given significance through social connections, when people feel that they are doing something which 'matters' to others, and when they feel that is recognised and appreciated.

Meaning is also amplified when we feel that we are not merely enjoying what we are doing and enjoying the company of others but are contributing to the common good, when we are making the world a better place.

CHAPTER 8

HOW SHOULD CHURCHES RESPOND?

A new Axial Age?

Before we examine how churches can and should respond to the changes in society that have been outlined in this book, it is helpful to put the rise of the churches into an historical perspective. The rise of the present forms in which our major religions exist can be traced to around 500 BCE when there were significant religious developments in several places around the world. It seems possible that this age of religion which had its origins 2,500 years ago may be coming to an end, and the secularisation process that has been outlined is part of a world-wide change of equal import. As we put it all into context, so we will summarise the major themes of this book.

As has been described well by Karen Armstrong in her book *The Great Transformation: The World in the Time of Buddha, Socrates, Confucius and Jeremiah*, most of the world's major religions have their origins in particular prophets or movements between 600 BCE and 500 BCE. Zoroastrianism was one of the first, arising from the teaching of Zoroaster in Iran between 624 and 599 BCE. He had some influence on the formation of Judaism and early Greek philosophers. Confucius began teaching in China around 500 BCE, teaching the importance of filial piety and respect for elders, seeing the family unit as the basis for social life. It is likely that Laozi, who is said to be the founder of Taoism, was teaching at a similar time, emphasising the importance of living in harmony with the principles of the universe.

Hinduism has very ancient origins in a great variety of local traditions in the Indian sub-continent. Some of ancient religious texts, the Vedas, may go back to 1500 BCE while some of the major Upanishads, which were philosophical reflections, were written around 800 BCE. About 600 BCE, Jainism was formed, introducing the idea of the spiritual goal of becoming liberated from the endless cycle of birth and re-birth. Less than one hundred years later, about 500 BCE, Siddhartha Gautama, known as the Buddha, developed his own philosophy, based on some components of Hinduism, but taking them in another direction, also suggesting how liberation from the cycle of birth and re-birth might occur.

Judaism also a long history which may go back to 1,800 BCE. However, most of its texts were written down and major developments occurred around 600 to 550 BCE when a large portion of the Jewish population was taken into Exile in the city of Babylon. The religious ideas were developed much further 550 years later with the teaching of Jesus. 600 years later again, Muhammad the prophet developed Islam. But what was important in the Jewish Exile was the development of small groups of people who were involved in writing down and reflecting on the religious texts. It was here that synagogues began, perhaps meeting on a weekly basis, rather than in the temple in Jerusalem and in a few other shrines for special holy days. The synagogues provided a pattern for the early Christian churches.

Also around 500 BCE, Socrates and Plato were teaching in Greece. Rather than focusing on the gods of Olympia, they developed new codes of ethics for personal life and new patterns for the government of society.

The German philosopher, Karl Jaspers coined the term 'Axial Age' for this period, an age around 500 BCE in which religious institutions began to develop separately from political institutions, and moral rules were developed separately from political authority.

It was a time of great reflection when a concept of history and a sense of an historical future developed. There have been various developments since. For example, between 1500 to 1600 CE when Protestantism split from Catholicism, with a new sense of authority built around the biblical texts rather than the church leaders. At a similar time, Sikhism developed in India, challenging the caste system and also developing faith and authority around a holy book, known as the *Guru Granth Sahib*. However, these future developments were not as momentous or as widespread in their occurrence as the initial Axial Age of Confucius in China, the Buddha in India, the Exilic prophets of Israel and Socrates and Plato in Greece.

There are many differences between these religions and philosophies. Most, but not all, supported a strong sense of duty to family and nation. Others focused more on inward development and finding inner peace. All of these religions supported gendered roles in the family and supported male leadership in their hierarchical forms of religious leadership. Confucius, the Buddha, Socrates and Plato all rejected the gods of their contemporaries while emphasising their new codes of conduct. The prophets of Israel, on the other hand, began to see their God, Yahweh, not just as the God of Israel but the God of the world and creator of the universe.

As social conditions have changed since World War II, particularly in the Western world, so we may be entering a new Axial Age. In this time of major change, religion in the forms that it has been in for centuries, even millennia, is in sharp decline and the lower levels of religiosity among younger people suggest that religions will continue to decline at least over the next fifty years. While it is likely that small groups of people will continue to celebrate the religious traditions for a very long time, the dominant ways of making sense of the world in which we live and the dominant values by which we live are changing.

The scientific method of developing knowledge has shown great strength. The strength is largely based on the fact that any assertion can be challenged and the evidence can be evaluated. New tests can be done and re-done. The rules about providing one's data so that it can be re-examined are being strengthened. The ways in which blind peer reviews of scientific work are conducted add to the strength of what is claimed as new knowledge. Science is not simply an ideology that is given from higher authorities; it is a method of seeking truth and is constantly evolving in its methods and in its findings. There are sceptics, as there is about every body of knowledge, but the ability to examine alternative theories and ideas means that scepticism can be overcome.

As we have examined what is beyond our earth, what the universe looks like, so we are constantly being amazed. So much of our knowledge of the universe has changed just in my lifetime. We are now aware of galaxies colliding and merging and galaxies going through a process of creation. Astronomers are now examining black holes and some of the roles they fill in the changing patterns of the universe as central components of the galaxies. From a human perspective, this all brings about a sense of the absolute enormity and complexity of the universe, and a sense of wonder at its mysteries.

Technology based on science has made huge practical advances. The ways in which we produce our food, build our shelters, and provide means of transport and communication, for example, have changed dramatically over my lifetime. I went to England to start my doctoral studies in 1978. It was that year that the first international direct dial telephones were introduced. I remember queueing at a library to use one to speak to my parents and friends back at home. It was a huge leap forward from the letters I used to write. And now I connect using video links with family and friends around the world: instant world-wide and cheap communication whenever we want it.

Great advances have been made in medical science. So much pain and suffering can be alleviated. Diseases can be cured. People who have lost their sight can be given back their sight. Diseases like smallpox which used to sweep through nations decimating numbers have almost been eliminated. Hearts, kidneys and other organs can be replaced. Again, many of these advances have occurred within my lifetime. Medical science cannot cure everything, but the knowledge base is continuing to grow and the range of medicines and forms of surgery available to use are continuing to increase. Where advanced medical facilities are available and affordable, people are living longer and with less pain and restriction than former generations.

As has been argued through this book, science in itself does not mean the end of religion, but it has replaced religion in a range of areas of knowledge and in a range of practical ways. Science provides a different picture of the universe and new ways of doing things, but in itself does not tell us how we should live.

Moral change has occurred in societies where there has been sufficient economic wellbeing to provide national safety nets for health, in times of disability and in aged care. In times when science has provided low infant mortality and control of fertility, combined with peace and economic prosperity, people have been able to turn their minds to seeking personal fulfilment as never before. Welfare systems have taken away some of the angst of personal existence, knowing that there are systems of care available in the difficult times of life. So people have been able to spend their time in pursuing health, enjoyment through sports, arts and culture, fulfilling relationships, interests and passions.

People find meaning in their enjoyment of life, in their many passions and interests, but particularly as these are shared with others. At the heart of meaning is the sense that we 'matter' to other people, we have something to contribute to the lives of other people, but also in the sense that they matter to us. So in relationships we find a sense of esteem and fulfilment, of belonging and of our lives having significance.

Relationships are built in a context of tolerance for difference, tolerance for people's different interests and ways of seeing and doing things. Relationships involve respect for others, for their cultures and backgrounds, and awareness of their wellbeing. As people interact with each other, they must do so seeking the other's consent, for it is important that we do not harm each other or limit their opportunities for finding personal fulfilment. Yet, together, we can find fulfilment in ways we cannot find alone. Even going for walks together is so much more fulfilling, very often, than walking alone.

Our activities for wellbeing include some which draw on ancient religious traditions. We draw on traditions of meditation, pilgrimage, yoga, and reflection in groups. We may be involved in music, singing and dancing, which draw on ancient patterns. What engages us depends on what we personally enjoy and find fulfilling, rather than on a set of duties and institutions into which we are born.

How churches should and should not respond

It can be hard to cope with the fading of religions and the decline of the religious institutions, particularly at the local level. People can certainly feel a deep sense of loss when doors are finally closed. The members lose their sense of community when churches cease to exist.

One of the challenges has been finding appropriate leadership in this time of decline. Most churches want leaders who will revive their churches, but the reality is that many ministers will inevitably oversee declining churches. In recent decades, some denominations have seen few people coming into ministry. Leadership of churches is not looking like a promising long-term occupation. Some denominations have turned to immigrants to fill the gaps. Thus, the 2021 Census showed that 49 per cent of all people whose primary occupation was the care of religious community and who identified as Catholic were born overseas as were 51 per cent of Seventh-day Adventist pastors and 48 per cent of Presbyterian and Reformed ministers. One third of all Uniting Church and Baptist ministers were also born overseas. Yet, importing people from different cultures to serve Australian-born congregations often works poorly. The problem is not just one of language, but of the expectations of each other and the customs and values that are not shared.

In 2008 and 2009, I looked at the issues of leadership in a number of rural places around Australia. Small rural churches were often the first to find they could neither afford leadership nor could they find people willing to go to isolated places. A variety of patterns emerged in various denominations. In the Catholic Church, I saw a rural church thriving when leadership had been given to an elected group of three women who undertook the pastoral work and led communion services on Sundays. A retired priest visited once a month to celebrate the Mass.

In another remote area of Australia, a team of lay people and clergy visited Anglican churches. They did not get to every church in the area every week, but they helped to keep these little communities of Anglicans alive, providing some pastoral care and conducting the sacraments.

Certainly, in rural areas, it has long been necessary to depend more on lay people than has occurred in the cities. Yet, even in the cities, finding fully trained, paid leadership has become increasingly difficult. Some solutions to this problem have proven not to work well and have contributed to the rapid decline of the church. The obvious solution for two small churches is to combine to become one church. The idea of merging churches is a good bureaucratic solution. However, it usually means people lose their sense of ownership and their sense of community. People give up their positions in the older community but do not always take on responsibility in the new community. It is easy to leave responsibilities to others. In general, the merging of congregations leads to smaller congregations and thus to faster decline.

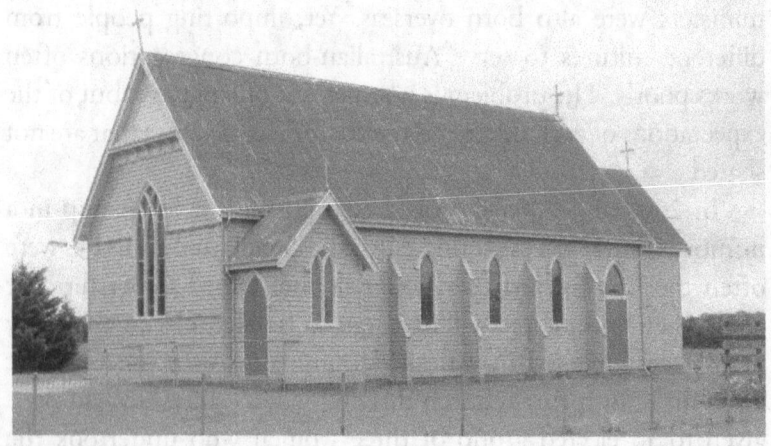

Rural churches were among the first to struggle to find professional leadership.

In a similar way, having a major church, often in a larger town, organising satellite churches did not prove to be very successful. When the local people did not have responsibility for what was happening in their churches, they lost a sense of agency and control, and eventually lost a sense of ownership, as can happen when churches are merged with each other.

The pattern we recommended for rural churches was having lay teams in each of the small churches, but having a 'team minister' who was responsible for the care and resourcing of the lay teams. The paid team minister would provide ideas and resources for services and other activities in the churches. He or she would also give support in ministry and help them to organise pastoral care.

It has been evident in the cities that the Protestant mega-churches, large churches of 1,000 or more members, have been attracting many people, many of them Pentecostal. In 2006, it was calculated that Melbourne had ten such mega-churches out of a total of 1,720 Protestant churches. Thus, the mega-churches represented just 0.6 per cent of all churches. However, of all people who attended a church monthly or more often, 20 per cent attended a mega-church. People are attracted by the professional quality of the music and the speakers, and the sense of being part of something much bigger than themselves.

One can go along to a mega-church and remain anonymous, if you want to. Cathedrals in England have continued to attract people, many of whom are visitors, curious about what is going on. Some of them have prayer boards where people can leave requests for prayer, giving some clues as to people's motivations in attending. Tania ap Siôn, Welsh sociologist, has analysed these requests and has argued that they show that there are many people on the fringes of the church, mostly wanting to remain anonymous, but looking for God to help them in a difficult situations, with health or with relationship challenges.

Mega-churches are attractive because they have facilities for all members of the family. They cater well for children and youth as well as the older members of the family. However, what keeps people involved in the long-term are the small groups where people do get to know each other and which can often evolve into a supportive gathering. Large churches only succeed long-term when they have an effective small group model. These small groups can be of various kinds. They may revolve around Bible study, but they can also be in the form of a book club or a mission group, a group which takes action such as environmental action, or a group which reflects together. In contemporary Western society, there is a need for diversity.

Small churches may also work well as a small group. It has been estimated that one can form close relations with around 20 people, while having some connection with 50 or more. In small churches, the Sunday service can provide a supportive community. The challenge for small churches is leadership and a location where they can meet. A group of 20 to 50 people cannot afford a full-time paid leader. They may also struggle to keep up with the maintenance of a church building. But there are other models using lay people and using hired property rather than owning a church building. They may also share leadership and property with another local church.

The churches which appear to be declining most rapidly are those churches of between 50 and 250 people. They neither have the advantages of the really large churches of highly professional music and speakers and a diversity of activities and small groups, but neither do they offer the warmth and intimacy of a small church.

As churches decline in size, there is a need to re-think what models are appropriate. A decade or more ago, Gary Bouma, a prominent sociologist and Anglican priest, argued that the era of religious professionals had come to an end. Certainly, in these times when individuals work out their own beliefs and sense of spirituality, many feel that they do not need a religious professional to tell them how to connect with God. Indeed, the 2018 *Australian Survey of Social Attitudes*, found that of all people who said they believed in God, at least sometimes, 66 per cent agreed with the statement "I have my own way of connecting with God without churches or religious services". Almost 40 per cent of those who were attending a church monthly or more often thought that way. While they attended a church, they did not feel that they **needed to** in order to connect with God.

Yet, every group, however large, needs someone to take initiative and ensure that the group meets. Most groups need leaders who can provide some music and inspiration. However, many groups find these among lay people who are not paid to lead. The Brethren, the Quakers, the Latter-day Saints have all relied on lay people who were not paid to lead their groups and to provide input into them.

Nor have these groups used expensive buildings. Buildings are all part of the institutionalism which is expensive and can draw more resources from human beings than the benefits they offer. On the other hand, many groups had made their church buildings work for them. I was very impressed by a 900 year old Anglican Church I visited in England. In one part of the church a play area had been developed and a couple of families were using it with their young children the afternoon I was there. In another part of the church was a cafe. There was no service when I visited and no other events happening, but the church was alive with people coming and going. It was evident that music concerts were held there. A large grand piano sat prominently in the central part of the church. A screen was stretched above the altar for singing or presentations. A LCD panel welcomed people and gave contact details. It was evident that the church was a central part of the community.

Some years ago, I looked at examples of where The Salvation Army combined facilities for their meetings with facilities for their services to the community. One particular example stood out. Among the services they offered was an employment centre where people could inquire about work opportunities. That centre often sent people down the corridor to the cafe where there were several computers. Volunteers at the cafe helped people to use the computers to find potential work. Young people were informed about the social gatherings of young people which the church organised. There was also a podiatrist operating from the facility catering mostly for older people. Again, the cafe provided the meeting place, and older people were informed about the social gatherings for older people. Another service offered within that one building was an opportunity or charity shop, again providing a place for connection with the wider community.

Another trend that I have noted is that people often connect with churches other than through the major times of worship. I first noted it many years ago when working with a church in a small rural town. The church had been given some land which could be farmed in order to raise money for a particular project. A number of people who never came to church had offered to farm the land. They wanted the church to be there. They supported the project. But they were not interested in coming to the Sunday services.

I saw the same thing with young people in a city context. These young people were very happy to be involved in a theatre program or in a music group, but were not interested in coming to the Sunday services. Sunday services attract some people but not others. Yet, they may well still be interested in being part of the church community. Churches need to open their side doors as well as their front doors to enable these people to be part of the community.

The importance of children and youth

Religious conversion is rare despite all the efforts that many churches and some other religious organisations put into trying to convert people and bring them into involvement in churches. In the 2018 *Australian Survey of Social Attitudes*, people were asked about church attendance when they were 11 years of age and about church attendance as adults at the time of the survey. Of those who never attended a church at 11 years of age, just 2 per cent were attending as adults. A few more (6%) who had just attended occasionally as a child were attending more frequently as adults. However, of all those who were attending monthly or more often as adults, 85 per cent had been attending at that frequency as children.

As has been seen, the major trend is towards attending less frequently. Thus, of those who had attended frequently as children, just 24 per cent had maintained that level of involvement, while 33 per cent were attending occasionally, and 43 per cent were not attending at all. Attendance as a child certainly did not guarantee attendance as an adult. On the other hand, not attending as a child made it very unlikely one would attend as an adult.

The primary means by which faith has been transmitted has been via the family supported by the religious community. If there is one thing which is most likely to slow the process of secularisation it is the development of patterns in family life which support the transmission of faith, accompanied by supportive patterns in the religious community.

At the 2023 conference of the International Society for the Sociology of Religion in Taipei, Peter Beyer, a prominent Canadian sociologist, argued that few people come into religious traditions in adulthood. Thus, conversions are not sufficiently frequent to counter the trend of secularisation. The one factor which is slowing the process of secularisation is successful transmission of religious faith in families. Beyer has been leading a team which has been conducting a major study both in Canada and in several countries in Europe looking at the transmission of faith. The team has followed a number of families over several decades and across several generations and in several countries, examining how successful the transmission of faith has been from grandparents to parents to children.

In general terms, the study has noted that the levels of religiosity were generally higher among evangelical Christians and Muslims, and lower among Catholics and mainstream Protestants. However, Beyer argued that successful transmission did occur sometimes in progressive mainstream religious families.

The team has found that 'strictness' in the religious group and in the family was not effective in ensuring there is successful transmission of faith, although it has been touted in the past as a potentially important factor. They also found that where there was a high level of competitiveness among churches that did not ensure successful transmission as Rodney Stark and others have argued.

In many families, a central parenting goal is the autonomy of the child. The child is encouraged to make his or her own decisions about faith. However, many young people find faith less and less plausible as they struggle to find a stable peer community which is committed to faith. Close families often encourage personal choice; and thus the closeness does not necessarily lead to successful transmission of faith.

What does make a difference is first of all the homogeneity of the family in terms of religion. If both parents are committed and are involved in religious practices in the home such as mealtime and bedtime prayers and in singing Christian songs in the home, that makes a difference. In addition, being part of a Christian community where there are children's services, confirmation classes and vibrant youth groups makes a difference. To the extent that children and young people are immersed in a sub-culture of people committed to faith, socialisation into faith is likely to be more successful.

Beyer's report echoed the findings of a large project on youth ministry in the USA published in 2010: *The Spirit and Culture of Youth Ministry* by R. Martinson, W. Black and J. Roberto. This study noted that the churches which were most successful in retaining their young people were those in which the whole church assisted in ministry among young people, with many adults building strong relationships with the young people and providing support for them.

While successful transmission of faith can slow the processes of secularisation, Beyer noted that this will not be sufficient to reverse the processes of secularisation. Even where the indicators pointed to transmission of faith likely to be successful, it was only successful in some cases. The long-term trend is that more people are dissociating from churches and from religion in general than are coming into the churches or other religious organisations.

However, a local church which is committed to its young people, has effective children's ministry and a vibrant small group culture, and uses its buildings well and lay leadership effectively will slow the rate secularisation.

Characteristics of being church

Secularisation is not just about the decline in church attendance, but the decline of the place of the churches, and of religion in general, in the wider society. Secularisation has to do with how the churches relate to the wider society and how the society perceives the churches. In the past, at times, they have played an important prophetic role. Groups of Christians, inspired by their faith, led the fight against slavery in Britain and colonies in the early 19th century, for example. There is a real prophetic role that the churches can and do play today. They do draw attention to the ways in which the focus on personal fulfilment can slide into selfishness. They do play a role in balancing consumerism with the wellbeing of the society. They highlight the importance of compassion for the vulnerable members of society. They do point towards the need to work for justice rooted in the equality of all human beings. On the other hand, faced with decline, many churches are focusing more on their inner life than on justice and wellbeing in the wider society.

At the moment, the churches are restrained in their effectiveness because they have lost the confidence of the wider society. As was noted in chapter 4, the proportion of the population in Australia with much confidence in the churches fell from 22 to 11 per cent just between 2009 and 2018. In a variety of ways, the churches have caused offence, and winning back the confidence of people will take a very special effort if it is to happen at all.

There is an underlying principle in early Christian teaching that, while we should be faithful to our faith and those things that are fundamental to us, to what is right and wrong, we should not give unnecessary offence to others. It is a principle that underlies the instructions in the first letter to Timothy (1 Timothy 2:1-2) where the author urges prayer for all those in authority "that we may all live peacefully and quiet lives in all godliness and holiness". It was this principle that led the writer of the letters to Timothy to recommend that women not lead in worship on the basis that this would cause offence in the wider society. However, in these days when the equality of men and women, the equality of people who are same-sex attracted and opposite-sex attracted, the equality of people with black skin and white skin, are seen as a fundamental value, some churches persist in giving offence by not allowing women in leadership for example. In most parts of the Western world, not giving equal opportunity for women to take leadership is seen as deeply morally offensive to the wider culture and to women generally.

As was noted in chapter four, the sexual abuse of others, and particularly of children, by people who were trusted to be moral leaders has been deeply offensive to society. Attempts to cover it up made it so much more offensive. Certainly some denominations have publicly lamented what has occurred and have sought to make recompense. But other denominations and religious bodies are still fighting the cases in the courts and still pretending they have done nothing wrong.

A recent essay by a barrister and member of the Anglican church, Leonie Bird (2024), analysing the situation in Melbourne, Australia, has noted that the ethical responsibility is not just to limit the possibility of future abuse, but to seek, as far as possible, the wellbeing of those who have been abused. The essay refers to the story of the Good Samaritan which Jesus told. Jesus presented the Good Samaritan as an ethical example. He not only rescued the person who had been beaten up by robbers (and who had been ignored by the religious officials) but paid for his care through to his recovery.

At the root of the teaching of Jesus was the model of serving others rather than trying to lord it over others. This is deeply rooted in the Christian tradition, and yet this is not what the public has always experienced. It is important that churches focus efforts on serving their communities and helping people to develop healthy relationships and communities, rather than opposition to certain forms of relationship such as same-sex marriage.

Analysis of the 2018 *Australian Survey of Social Attitudes* showed that another factor in the lack of confidence in the churches and religious organisations more generally was the affirmation by 72 per cent of all Australians that "Looking around the world, religions bring more conflict than peace". The only way this attitude will be overcome is if Christians re-double their efforts in truly seeking peace.

The misuse of power is sometimes seen in local churches as leaders attempt to control their members, to exert authority, and to close down debate. Research for a doctorate by Mark Bohr of young people who had ceased to attend church in Australia found many examples of this occurring. Young people were angry because there was no opportunity for opinions contrary to that of the leaders to be expressed. There are still pressures for members of some churches to conform to the opinions of the leaders.

An earlier study of why people do not attend church conducted by John Bellamy and a team of researchers in 1999 found that 16 per cent of Australians who had reduced the frequency of going to church said a major reason was bad experiences with other people in a church. Eleven per cent said such an experience was the major catalyst. The study concluded:

> People leave because they have been deeply offended by what someone has said or because they were not shown care in time a need. The ability to offer pastoral care to such people can make a difference in preventing the departure from church life. (Bellamy et al., p.103)

It is important that churches are tolerant of people and willing to listen rather than jumping in with specific advice. Lack of tolerance is certainly offensive to many people in the churches and in the wider community. It is important that churches reaffirm that their priority is service, not taking control. The emphasis on humble service is needed not just for winning the confidence of the current culture, but also for maintaining the essence of its own traditions.

It is also important for religious organisations to be sensitive to particular ethical issues which concern the wider population. Today, one pressing ethical issue is that of the environment and climate change. Already, millions of people are suffering from more extreme heat, droughts and fires, storms, floods and landslides due to the warming planet. The warming is affecting plants and animals and the general bio-diversity on the planet. Without very significant action, the problems could become very much worse and whole populations would be affected. Yet, as has been noted earlier, on the whole, while many denominations have made statements about environmental concerns, Stephen Reid has shown in recent analysis of Australian survey data, church attenders are expressing less concern about environmental issues than those who never attend. Again, this is an issue which lowers the level of confidence in the churches and shows that they are not on the forefront of the moral issues for our society.

An emerging ethical issue in the Western world is the treatment of animals, from whales to pets, from animals in zoos to animals in farms. Realising that animals can suffer just as humans can is leading people to review how we treat animals. For some, it has meant adopting a vegan diet. That ethical issue is yet to make it onto the agenda of most churches.

One ministry which is working in many places is chaplaincy where chaplains work in hospitals, prisons, sporting clubs, schools and other places. As a primary model, chaplaincy involves working with individuals, forming relationships and giving support to people. It usually happens in a non-denominational way, so chaplains work with people whatever their religious backgrounds. They are there to support and not judge. In his recent doctoral thesis on the effectiveness of sport chaplains, Stephen Reid found that there was often some suspicion of them at first, but as chaplains got to know people and showed that they were not about making converts but were there to be supportive, they won respect and people gained confidence in them. A similar pattern was evident in a study of chaplaincy in government-run schools. Their pattern was different from that of professional psychologists and counsellors in that they formed relationships first. They were often then the first port of call for those experiencing some personal issues or challenges. They could refer people on to the psychologists if the issues were more than could be solved through friendship and support.

Resources for nurturing the spirit and creating community

In coming decades, churches will continue to serve a small sector of the population. The immigrant churches will serve their immigrant populations. Conservative and charismatic churches will serve the small portion of the population which appreciates the focus on family life.

The great challenge for the churches is whether they focus on serving the 10 per cent of people who attend, or whether they will seek to have positive engagement with the 90 per cent of people who do not. Apart from chaplaincy, there are other ways in which churches might connect with people in the wider society for whom church services are no longer relevant. If the aim of the churches is to help people find a sense of meaning, they can well do it through creating the sorts of communities in which people find meaning. However, to do that, we need to look briefly at changes in the patterns of organisations.

There are significant differences between the organisations which are important to those who grew up in the era of duty and those who have grown up in the era of personal fulfilment. Those who have grown up in the era of personal fulfilment, since World War II, have not only left the churches, but have diminished their involvement in many other groups. They are not as active in the social service groups such as Rotary and Lions, nor in general social clubs such as Senior Citizens. Political parties have found it harder in more recent years to recruit members. People are general slower to commit themselves to groups which have general aims and activities, which are there simply for providing social connection or for general social service.

More work needs to be done to determine more precisely the causes of these changes. However, there appear to be several factors. One is related to that sense of personal fulfilment, which takes quite specific forms in most people. Thus, people will look for activities which relate specifically to their sense of personal fulfilment rather than simply looking for a general group with a variety of activities which provides social connection or social service. Thus, people may connect with a group which is involved with landcare in their own area, or keeps a bike-track they use clear of weeds, rather than a group which seeks in general ways to serve the local area. They will look for a group which meets to play mahjong, or goes to see films together, rather than a general social group.

Higher levels of formal education and more specific ways of engaging in the workforce have led people to look for particular ways in which to find personal fulfilment. One example of that is the proliferation of sporting clubs. Up until the 1950s, most Australians played football (of one kind or another) in winter and cricket in summer (with a few playing tennis). If you were an older person, you might play bowls. One went to the sporting ground that was within walking distance. As families purchased their first and then second car, they lived in more extended communities, and the sporting options multiplied. Today, there are thousands of options for sport and people pick and choose the option that most attracts them or suits them. There are options at the beach with beach volleyball and surfing as well as swimming. There are options in the high country in the snow season. There are options in the various clubs around the suburbs. As people look for the specific sport that engages them, so they look for the specific activities and social connections through which they might find personal fulfilment.

Along with this proliferation of activities, people are generally suspicious of hierarchical or controlling situations. They want to participate on their own terms, as is helpful to their personal fulfilment. They want freedom to come and go. Most people are balancing a range of activities and responsibilities, in family, work and leisure. They want the option of travelling, of looking after the relative who needs special care, of simply taking time off to do something else.

U3A is one of the communities which, in many places, is thriving. One of its strengths is that it offers a great range of options in which people can get involved. One chooses the classes that are of interest, whether it be family history or film making, singing or learning Spanish. One makes limited commitments, usually for just one term or semester. There are options for giving as well as receiving. Thus, members are invited to run classes as well as attend those run by others. Many neighbourhood houses seem to be doing well working on similar principles.

The organisational patterns of U3A may provide some clues as to how churches might engage with the wider population. It may offer opportunities for discussion on specific topics, or action groups which engage with specific issues. It can also bring people together to take action on the environment, such as a repair café. It can organise housing for the homeless or food for the hungry. There are many charitable organisations which have their origins in the churches which are doing such things today, but sometimes they have become separated from the local communities and less able to offer a sense of community through their services. Churches can offer theatre and choirs, pilgrimages and opportunities for meditation. They can offer music concerts and art as ways in which people may find nurture for their sense of spirit.

There is a place for large gatherings, but when church life is focused on Sunday services which are meant to suit everyone, 90 per cent of Australians are not interested. About 2005, I was involved in a small local church. We had about 75 people on our membership list and about 45 people in church on a typical Sunday. We decided to establish a Community Living Centre as a way of engaging people in the local community. We invited people to run programs such as yoga and meditation. We had a book club. Every week, there was a casual coffee shop on a Wednesday afternoon. There was a group learning how to play pool, and another group learning a language. There was a belly-dancing group too. One group which was quite popular was Focus on Faith, led by the minister of the church. We advertised these activities through a newsletter which was distributed through all the homes in the local area. We charged a sufficient rate for attending these various activities to cover the cost of a part-time co-ordinator and the cost of the facilitators of the various activities. Through these activities, we had two aims: to nurture the spirit and to build community. It was not long at all before we had many more people involved in these activities than came to church on Sunday mornings.

Our small Sunday morning congregation became nervous, however, when the minister retired. They could not see it as possible to find a new minister and did not believe they could find the money to afford someone. They merged with another church and the property was sold. The Community Living Centre was moved to the new church. But it was not supported and there were lots of restrictions on the use of the buildings of the new church. The Community Living Centre closed after eleven years of operation. We also became aware of much competition from neighbourhood houses working on similar principles.

Yet, quite a number of the activities continued in various ways. The book group continued to meet for many years. The yoga class was transferred to another church, and then eventually to a neighbourhood house. The group which played pool continued for several more years in the home of the facilitator.

While the Community Living Centre eventually ceased operating, I think the model contained some keys for how churches may engage the wider community. It recognised that there are many ways through which the spirit can be nurtured and community can be grown. It did not require people to become members first and then invite them into a group. Rather, the doors were opened to the wider public, allowing them to come in. The activities required just a short-term commitment, rather than beginning with the expectation that people would come every week for the rest of their lives.

There are now many other places in our communities where similar activities are occurring, mostly outside the churches. People gather informally at coffee shops or participate in meditation. They engage with each other as part of a cycling group, or play pickleball together. They volunteer to provide food and shelter for the homeless, or support asylum seekers. At the same time, as the well-known Australian social commentator and researcher, Hugh Mackay, has pointed in his book *The Way We Are*, there is an epidemic of loneliness. People are finding it hard to make meaningful connections with each other and this is feeding the mental health crisis in Australia and in other Western countries.

While fewer are attending Sunday services, there are a thousand other ways in which the spirit is being nurtured and community is being built. It behoves each individual to contribute as they are able: to find ways where they can nurture the spirit of others and can create community. Underlying these activities must be the basic assumptions of inclusion of all people. Indeed, we recognise that building community across the boundaries of race and class, education and age, gender and language is vital to creating cohesive community. At the same time, we recognise that the tolerance of difference must be within the bounds that we do not harm each other, and we engage each other with respect seeking consent for our interactions.

We may not use the language of faith within these contexts. Indeed, we may have some quite different ideas about the origin of the universe and what holds it in existence. We may have some different ideas about what happens after people die. We may discuss these ideas, but will do so with humility, recognising that these metaphysical elements of 'Truth' are beyond human knowledge and comprehension. Yet, in our common humanity, as we seek to live in peace and harmony with each other, and are inspired to find that peace and harmony within ourselves, so the Spirit of Love will prevail.

References

ap Siôn, Tania, (2013) 'Ordinary Prayer and the Activity of God: Reading a Cathedral Prayer Board' in Jeff Astley and Lesley J. Francis (editors) *Exploring Ordinary Theology: Explorations in practical and empirical theology*, Ashgate, Aldershot.

Armstrong, Karen. (2006) *The Great Transformation: The World in the Time of Buddha, Socrates, Confucius and Jeremiah*. Great Britain: Atlantic Books.

Australian Bureau of Statistics (2024) Schools: Data on government and non-government students, staff and schools. (https://www.abs.gov.au/statistics/people/education/schools/latest-release)

Bellamy, John, Alan Black, Keith Castle, Philip Hughes, and Peter Kaldor. (2002) *Why People Don't Go to Church*. Adelaide: Openbook.

Berger, Peter. (1992) *A Far Glory*. New York: Doubleday.

Bird, Leonie. (2024) 'The Lawyer's Question, the Law of Negligence and the Parable of the Good Samaritan'. *Journal of Contemporary Ministry* 9:68–100.

Bohr, Mark and Philip Hughes, (2021) 'Why Gen Y are Leaving Hillsong and Other Pentecostal Churches', *Journal of Contemporary Ministry* 5:10-30.

Bouma, Gary. (2006) *Australian Soul: Religion and Spirituality in the Twenty-first Century*. Melbourne: Cambridge University Press.

Brown, Andrew, and Linda Woodhead. (2016) *That Was the Church That Was: How the Church of England Lost the English People*. London: Bloomsbury Publishing.

Carrette, Jeremy R., and Richard King. (2005) *Selling Spirituality: The Silent Takeover of Religion*. London; New York: Routledge.

Commonwealth of Australia. (2017) *Royal Commission into Institutional Responses to Child Sexual Abuse: Final Report*. Sydney: Commonwealth of Australia.

Damon, William. (2008) *The Path to Purpose: Helping Our Children Find Their Calling in Life*. New York: Free Press.

Dantis, Trudy, Stephen Reid, Leith Dudfield and Katherine Jelavic (2024) *The Australian Catholic Mass Attendance Report 2021*. Canberra: National Centre for Pastoral Research. https://ncpr.catholic.org.au/national-count-of-attendance/

Day, Abby. (2011) *Believing in Belonging: Belief and Social Identity in the Modern World*. Oxford: Oxford University Press.

Dobbelaere, Karel. (2007) 'Secularization', in *The Blackwell Encyclopedia of Sociology*, edited by George Ritzer, 1st ed. Wiley. https://doi.org/10.1002/9781405165518.wbeoss064

Finke, Roger, and Rodney Stark. (1992) *The Churching of America, 1776-1990: Winners and Losers in Our Religious Economy*. New Brunswick, N.J: Rutgers University Press.

Flett, Gordon L. (2018) *The Psychology of Mattering: Understanding the Human Need to Be Significant*. London, United Kingdom; San Diego, CA: Academic Press, an imprint of Elsevier.

Francis, Niel. (2021) *Religiosity in Australia*. Melbourne: Rationalist Society of Australia. https://rationalist.com.au/religiosity-in-australia/

Geels, Antoon. (2009) 'Global Spirituality' in T. Ahlbäck and B. Dhala, *Postmodern Spirituality*, Åbo, Finland: Donner Institute for Research in Religious and Cultural History.

Heelas, Paul, and Linda Woodhead. (2005) *The Spiritual Revolution: Why Religion Is Giving Way to Spirituality*. Oxford: Blackwell Publishing.

Hughes, P. and Bond, S., Bellamy, J. and Black, A. (2003) *Exploring What Australians Value*, Adelaide: Open Book Publishers.

Hughes, Philip. (2007) *Putting Life Together: Findings from Australian Youth Spirituality Research*. Melbourne: Fairfield Press.

Hughes, Philip, Alan Black, Peter Kaldor, John Bellamy and Keith Castle. (2007) *Building Stronger Communities*. Sydney: University of New South Wales Press.

Hughes, Philip. (2013) 'Spirituality and Religious Tolerance'. *Journal of Implicit Religion* 16 (1): 65–91.

Hughes, Philip, and Lachlan Fraser. (2014) *Life, Ethics and Faith in Australian Society: Facts and Figures*. Melbourne: Christian Research Association.

Hughes, Philip. (2023) 'Re-Building Confidence as a Prelude to Ministry'. *Journal of Contemporary Ministry* 7: 7–30.

Inglehart, Ronald. (2021) *Religion's Sudden Decline: What's Causing It, and What Comes Next?* New York, NY: Oxford University Press.

Kaldor, Peter, Philip Hughes, and Alan Black. (2010) *Spirit Matters: How Making Sense of Life Affects Wellbeing*. Melbourne: Mosaic Press.

Klein, Stefan. (2014) *Survival of the Nicest: How Altruism Made Us Human and Why It Pays to Get Along*. London: Scribe Publications.

Kasselstrand, Isabella, Phil Zuckerman, and Ryan T. Cragun. (2023) *Beyond Doubt: The Secularization of Society*. Secular Studies. New York: New York University Press.

Kruithoff, Uwe. (2023) 'Factors influencing monoethnic churches' longevity'. Doctor of Ministry Thesis, Alphacrucis University College.

Mackay, Hugh (2024) *The Way We Are: Lessons from a lifetime of listening*. Sydney: Allen & Unwin.

Martin, David. (1978) *A General Theory of Secularization*. Oxford: Basil Blackwell.

Martinson, Roland, Wes Black, and John Roberto. (2010) *The Spirit and Culture of Youth Ministry: Leading Congregations Towards Exemplary Youth Ministry*. St Paul, Minnesota, United States: Exemplary Youth Ministry Publishing.

Mason, Michael, Andrew Singleton and Ruth Webber (2007) *The Spirit of Generation Y: Young people's spirituality in a changing Australia*. Melbourne: John Garrat Publishing.

Mol, Hans. (1985) *The Faith of Australians*. Sydney: Allen and Unwin.

NCLS Research. (undated) What Types of Social Services Do Local Churches Provide? https://www.ncls.org.au/articles/what-types-of-social-services-do-local-churches-provide/

Porter, Muriel. (2015) *A New Exile? The future of Anglicanism.* Melbourne: Morning Star Publishing.

Prilleltensky, Isaac, and Ora Prilleltensky. (2021) *How People Matter: Why It Affects Health, Happiness, Love, Work, and Society.* Cambridge, United Kingdom; New York, NY: Cambridge University Press.

Rawlings, Helen (2006) *The Spanish Inquisition.* Malden, MA, USA: Blackwell Publishing.

Reid, Stephen (2022) 'Changes in Australians' Concern for the Environment.' *Pointers: Bulletin of the Christian Research Association* 32(1), pp. 14-15.

Reid, Stephen. (2024) 'Ministry on Their Turf: The Roles and Functions of Christian Sports Chaplains in Contemporary Australian Society'. *Journal of Contemporary Ministry* 9: 192–234.

Schnell, Tatjana. (2021) *The Psychology of Meaning in Life.* London; New York: Routledge.

Smith, Christian, and Melinda Lundquist Denton. (2005) *Soul Searching: The Religious and Spiritual Lives of American Teenagers.* Oxford: Oxford University Press.

Stark, Rodney and William Sims Bainbridge. (1996) *A Theory of Religion.* New Brunswick, New Jersey: Rutgers University Press.

Thompson, A. K., ed. (2023) *The Economic Impact of Religion on Society in Australia: Recent Research and Commentary.* Cleveland, Qld: Shepherd Street Press.

Voas, David and Steve Bruce. (2007). 'The Spiritual Revolution: Another False Dawn for the Sacred'. In K. Flanagan and

P. Jupp, *A Sociology of Spirituality*, Farnham, Surrey: Ashgate, pp. 43-62.

Voas, David, and Stefanie Doebler. (2011) 'Secularization in Europe: Religious Change between and within Birth Cohorts'. *Religion and Society in Central and Eastern Europe* 4(1): 39–62.

White, L, (1967) 'The historical roots of our ecological crisis', *Science* 155, pp. 1203-1207.

Wong, Paul. (2011) 'Positive Psychology 2.0: Towards a Balanced Interactive Model of the Good Life'. *Canadian Psychology*, 52(2), pp.69-81.

Data Used and Referred to in This Book

Australian Bureau of Statistics (2022) *2021 Census of Population and Housing*, Canberra.
Most of the data was obtained through the use of TableBuilder on the website of the Australian Bureau of Statistics which allows people to build their own tables from the Census data from the 2006, 2011, 2016, and 2021 censuses. Note that much of the Census data report in this book was first reported in Hughes, Philip (2022) *Australia's Religious and Non-religious Profiles: Analysis of the 2021 Census Data*. Melbourne: Christian Research Association.

Australian Bureau of Statistics (2022) *Australian Census Longitudinal Data Set*, Canberra. This sub-set of data from the 2006, 2011 and 2016 censuses has been incorporated into TableBuilder allowing people to build their own tables and conduct their own analyses.

Christian Research Association (2016) *Contributing to Australian Society Survey*. Melbourne: Christian Research Association. This survey was commissioned by the Study of the Economic Impact of Religion on Society (SEIROS).

Evans, Ann (2019) *Australian Survey of Social Attitudes* 2018. (Computer file) Canberra: Australian National University.

ADDITIONAL READING

Websites. For the most recent data and research, go to:

www.cra.org.au - the website of the Christian Research Association which has produced a wide range of materials analysing Census data, data from the Australia Survey of Social Attitudes and its own survey such as the Contributing to Australian Society survey;

www.ncls.org.au – the website of NCLS Research which has been conducting major surveys of churches throughout Australia since 1991 and has conducted major studies of the Australian community since 1998;

https://ncpr.catholic.org.au/ - the website of the National Centre for Pastoral Research, which has contains detailed research relating to the Catholic Church in Australia.

Note that the most detailed recent data on religion in Australia is contained in:
Hughes, Philip. *Australia's Religious and Non-religious Profiles: Analysis of the 2021 Census Data*. Christian Research Association, 2022.

Books.

Bellamy, John, Alan Black, Keith Castle, Philip Hughes, and Peter Kaldor. (2002) *Why People Don't Go to Church*. Adelaide: Openbook. Based on data gathered in 1998 when 20 per cent of the population attended a church, this book analyses at depth the reasons people gave at that time for ceasing to attend.

Bouma, Gary D. (2006) *Australian Soul: Religion and Spirituality in the 21st Century*. Melbourne: Cambridge University Press. This is a major book on the nature of religion in Australia, noting its 'low temperature' compared with many other countries.

Robert Dixon. (2018) 'Post-Secularity and Australian Catholics', in Anthony Maher (ed), *Faith and the Political in the Post Secular Age*. Bayswater: Coventry Press. An analysis of trends in the Catholic Church in the light of theories of secularisation and post-secularity.

Frame, Tom. (2009) *Losing My Religion: Unbelief in Australia*. Sydney: UNSW Press. A description of the rise of 'no religion' and its significance for Australian society.

Hughes, Philip, Craig Thompson, Rohan Pryor, and Gary D Bouma. (1995) *Believe It or Not: Australian Spirituality and the Churches in the 90s*. Melbourne: Christian Research Association. Based on data gathered in 1993 and 1994, the book describes the diversity of different forms of spirituality which were being explored at the time and analyses why some people were looking outside the churches for spiritual resources.

Hughes, Philip (editor) (2010) *Australia's Religious Communities: A Multimedia Exploration*. (CD-Rom 3rd edition) Melbourne: Christian Research Association. Three editions were created of this encyclopedic work on religion in Australia covering the 30 major religious groups in depth and an additional 150 groups in profile, along with general materials on the history and nature of religion in Australia.

Hughes, Philip. (2016) *Charting the Faith of Australians: Thirty Years in the Christian Research Association*, Melbourne: Christian Research Association. The story in this book is how the change in nature of religion in Australia was charted over 30 years from 1985 to 2015 and what the overall pattern looked like in 2015. It also contains a full list of publications produced by the staff of the Christian Research Association up to that point.

Jupp, James. (2009) *The Encyclopedia of Religion in Australia*. Melbourne: Cambridge University Press. A comprehensive book covering every aspect of religion in Australia.

Kaldor, Peter, John Bellamy, Ruth Powell, Merilyn Correy, and Keith Castle. (1994) *Winds of Change: The Experience of Church in a Changing Australia*. Sydney: Lancer. A major book based on the National Church Life Survey of 1991 looking in detail at the nature of local church life how the churches were navigating the increasingly turbulent times of change.

Mackay, Hugh. (2016) *Beyond Belief: How we find meaning without religion*. Australia: Macmillan. From a leading Australian social researcher, this book explores how belief in God is waning, but how people are exploring a sense of meaning in a great variety of ways. Unlike most other books, Hugh Mackay uses focus groups and interviews rather than surveys for gathering his data.

Mol, Hans. (1985) *The Faith of Australians*. Sydney: Allen and Unwin. A classic book which contains data from 1966 showing what religion in Australia was like prior to the major changes of the 1970s and beyond.

Rose, Gerald, Gary D. Bouma, and Philip Hughes. (2014) *Re-Imagining the Church*. Melbourne: Christian Research Association. This book argues that the major change in Australian religion has been from dogma to experience. It draws pictures of various ways in which churches are being expressed in this new age.

Secularisation.

Note that the two books which, in the opinion of the author of this book, best describe the most recent data and theory of secularisation at a world-wide level are:

Inglehart, Ronald. (2021) *Religion's Sudden Decline: What's Causing It, and What Comes Next?* New York, NY: Oxford University Press.

Kasselstrand, Isabella, Phil Zuckerman, and Ryan T. Cragun. (2023) *Beyond Doubt: The Secularization of Society*. Secular Studies. New York: New York University Press.

There is a huge literature on secularisation. Some useful books include the following.

Berger, Peter L. (1973) *The Social Reality of Religion*. Middlesex, England: Penguin Books. Original published in 1967 as *The Sacred Canopy*, this is a classic text on secularisation. Berger later came to reject the theory, but much in his description of how religion operates in society remains valid.

Groot, Kees de. (2018) *The Liquidation of the Church*. Routledge New Critical Thinking in Religion, Theology, and Biblical Studies. New York: Routledge, Taylor & Francis Group. Written in the Netherlands by a Dutch sociologist, this is a helpful account of the process of secularisation which includes reference to some of the intermediate steps in the process including the emergence of chaplaincy.

Hughes, Philip. (2017) *Educating for Purposeful Living in a Post-Traditional Age*. Christian Research Association. Suggests ways in which religious education in secondary schools might be adapted for a more secular age.

Ireland, Rowan. (1988) *The Challenge of Secularisation*. Australia: Collins Dove. An early book on secularisation, relating particularly to Australia.

Luckmann, Thomas. (1967) *The Invisible Religion*. New York: Macmillan. An early classic text on contemporary secularisation and the privatisation of religion.

Singleton, Andrew. (2014) *Religion, Culture and Society: A Global Approach*. Los Angeles: SAGE. A most helpful and accessible account of the various theories of secularisation and their strengths and weaknesses.

www.ingramcontent.com/pod-product-compliance
Lightning Source LLC
Chambersburg PA
CBHW011150290426
44109CB00025B/2559